Doing
Business
with the
Japanese

For the late W O Dickins in gratitude

Doing
Business
with the
Japanese

John A S Abecasis-Phillips

NTC Business Books
a division of *NTC Publishing Group* • Lincolnwood, Illinois USA

The masculine pronoun has been used throughout this book. This stems from a desire to avoid ugly and cumbersome language, and no discrimination, prejudice or bias is intended.

Library of Congress Cataloging-in-Publication Data

Abecasis-Phillips, J. A. S. (John Andrew Stephen), 1934-
    Doing business with the Japanese / John A.S. Abecasis-Phillips.
        p.   cm.
    Includes bibliographical references and index.
    ISBN 0-8442-8392-4
    1. Japan--Economic conditions--1945- 2. Corporate culture--Japan.
  3. Investments, Foreign--Japan. 4. Corporations, Foreign--Japan.
  5. Intercultural communication.   I. Title.
  HC462.9.A6417   1993
  306'.0952--dc20   93-421
                                                                        CIP

Published in the United States in 1994 by NTC Business Books,
a division of NTC Publishing Group 4255 West Touhy Avenue,
Lincolnwood (Chicago), Illinois 60646-1975, U.S.A.
©1992 by John A S Abecasis-Phillips. All rights reserved.
No part of this book may be reproduced, stored in a retrieval system,
or transmitted in any form or by any means, electronic, mechanical,
photocopying, recording or otherwise, without the prior permission
of NTC Publishing Group.
This edition first published in the United Kingdom in 1992 by Kogan
Page, 120 Pentonville Road, London N1 9JN.
Manufactured in the United States of America.

3 4 5 6 7 8 9 0 VP 9 8 7 6 5 4 3 2 1

Contents

Part II   Doing Business with Japan Abroad

Preface

This is not a manual for doing business with the Japanese, but a guide to understanding what is going on behind the seemingly inscrutable face of the Japanese. Although not a manual, it has a practical purpose as a companion designed to help the reader avoid some of the frustration often experienced by the beginner. This book is written by neither an expert nor businessman, but an observer who has been intimately involved in the intricacies of Japanese decision-making processes and cross-cultural considerations which at first so mystify foreigners.

Doing business with the Japanese is not simply doing business, but something more. The Japanese concept of business is itself different from the word in the Western sense. Profit is only part of the story. This book attempts to deal with the rest. It is primarily about the struggle for growth, that is market growth without cornering the market in such a way as to bust it. Japanese domestic market harmony has to be preserved literally at all costs. For a foreigner this is a key factor in understanding how to do business with the Japanese on their own ground. Globally, other factors obtain. No doubt the reader of this book is interested in trying to enter the Japanese home market of 123 million people, the second largest sophisticated market in the world, but often considered the most difficult. It is estimated that a seventh of foreign ventures in Japan fail.

The purpose of this book is to make the prospect less daunting without suggesting that there is a neat formula to fit every situation. At the most it can offer hints and guidelines, but these will not be infallible. There are many similarities but also many differences to be considered in doing business with the Japanese. Undoubtedly the best advice is what the Japanese advocate in every available situation: *ganbatte* (keep trying), to which I would add 'be prepared'. And preparation is the subject of the first chapter of this book.

Acknowledgements

My first debt of gratitude is to President Yoshiyasu Shirai of the University of Osaka Gakuin, which hosted me as a visiting lecturer from October 1989 to September 1991 during my sabbatical from the University of Bayreuth whose President, Dr Klaus Dieter Wolff kindly granted me the first year and then with the approval of the Bavarian Ministry of Education, Science and Culture, the second. In the latter connection I wish to express my gratitude to Ministerialdirigent Grote who has always been so supportive of my writing. I should also like to thank Professor Dr P R Wossidlo, of the Law and Commerce Department at Bayreuth University who morally supported my project, especially the appropriate extension of my sabbatical from 2 to 4 years. Ministerialdirigent Grote and President Dr Klaus Dieter Wolff then approved this extension after my supervisor, Dr Udo O Jung, Administrative Director of the Bayreuth University Language Centre had very kindly agreed to arrange for a substitute during my absence. Professor Dr Walter Breu, Academic Director of the Language Centre, very kindly supported my sabbatical in the first place.

In Japan, Osaka Gakuin University not only paid my salary, but also generous research allowances which included a large annual sum for books. To the librarians Kakitani, Katsuyoshi Esq, Ms Takako, INOUE, Ms Hisako Fukatani, Ms Yuko Goto, Ms Misa Hirooka, Ms Yuriko Yano and Ms Rika Okajima who were all extremely kind and patient, I extend my heartfelt thanks, especially when I was allowed to retain loan of the books after my contract with the University had run out. The free use of Xerox copying facilities was another great boon, as was the assistance I received in working the machines, which were being renewed at the time, from the following kind ladies: Ms Kazue Murakami, Ms Yuka Hirose, Ms Kumi Ishikawa, Ms Akiko Iwamoto, Ms Sachiko Kakunaka, and Ms Hiromi Takeda, especially Ms Tomoko Tsumura. They were the soul of patience and charming with it too, thus relieving me of a great deal of tedious work so that I could get on with writing the book. Osaka Gakuin taught me how a Japanese organization (a private family university) works, and for that I remain immensely grateful. (A Japanese university is a microcosm of Japanese society, from the dignified President at the top down to the cleaner bowing respectful early morning greetings at the bottom, to which for two wonderful years I was privileged to belong, having, I suspect, unwittingly tested everybody's patience.) They are all in this book or were in my mind as I wrote it. Many thanks.

For help with the subject matter, I should like to thank the following for giving of their time: P H Gee, Esq, of Lloyd's Register, Tokyo; Michael I Gourlay, Esq, Manager for Royal Insurance, Japan; Graham M Harris Esq, Area Director, Lloyds Bank, Japan; Gordon Nebeker, Esq, Director of N M Rothschild & Sons Ltd, Japan; Christopher T B Purvis, Esq, Branch Manager, S G Warburg Securities (Japan) Inc, Tokyo Branch; Kenichi Tsurutani Esq, Manager, Foreign Exchange Dept, The Dai-Ichi Kangyo Bank, Osaka Branch.

I would like to thank Martin Hood Esq, Assistant Manager at NatWest, Tokyo, for the trouble he took in trying to arrange an interview with the local director and for the advice he gave me in connection with the book. Richard Schofield, Esq, Vice-Chairman of The British Chamber of Commerce, Osaka, Robert Rayner Esq, British Consul (Commercial), Osaka, kindly answered questions.

For advice on Japanese culture and society, I am greatly indebted to Ms Manami Yasukochi, Ms Michiyo Nishizawa; Yoshiaki Ohta, Esq, and to Takao Oshima, Esq, Director and Chief Secretary, respectively, of The Japan–Sweden Society of Kansai; and especially to my former colleague Professor John Hodge of Osaka Gakuin University who explained to me many inexplicables over the telephone. Ditto Adrian Sydenham Esq, who gave me mini-lectures standing in the corridor. Otherwise much would have remained most unclear.

Of the Japanese who helped me (I cannot forget all the unknown people who sent me things on request), I should particularly like to mention Kondo Takashi Esq now at JETRO's Import Promotion Division in Tokyo, who went out of his way to help in answering questions, producing material and negotiating with his Tokyo headquarters to send me even more. Having studied in America, he had a wide vision of the problems with which I was confronted.

My thanks also go to Sandy Taubenkimel Esq, President of the International Business Association in Osaka. I learnt a lot from attending the monthly meetings at the Traveller's Vic in the magnificent New Otani Hotel and, as almost the only Englishman present among so many Americans, being able to listen to excellent speakers, question them and 'grill' the members afterwards. All were 'front line troops', individual entrepreneurs, and taught me about the realities of doing business with the Japanese.

Much about what it means to work as a Japanese *salaryman* in a typical Japanese company, I learnt from long weekend conversations with Takafumi Miyamoto Esq of Toshiba, who very kindly came down twice from Tokyo to help me with my computer and who very kindly suggested the loan of a larger computer so I could write this book on it. I also wish to thank Takao Sakamoto Esq, Manager at the International Department at Toshiba, for authorizing the loan and Declan Niall Esq, serving an internship from Ireland, who taught me, a complete computer novice, how to master it. My thanks to H Nakazawa Esq and his assistant Ms Imoto of Micro Pro who very kindly originally provided me with special adaptations of the WordStar 5 programme for my use.

I should particularly like to record my extreme debt of gratitude to Dr Hotoshi Kimura, President of Shujitsu Joshi University, my Dean, Professor Yoshio Katayama, and Professor Masami Fujii, Head of the English Department, who very kindly agreed to employ me as a University Lecturer, in the middle of the academic year when my contract with Osaka Gakuin ran out. The new post at Shujitsu Joshi was to have been filled from the beginning of the next academic year. Yet realizing my need, the University put forward the contract by six months. I was, therefore, able to stay in the country to finish this book under ideal conditions. To all at Shujitsu Joshi, my heartfelt thanks for so much kindness and understanding.

Writing a book about a foreign country while in that country, where you do not speak the language properly nor read it, places a great burden upon your conscience as well as your native wit. I think I learnt a lot by simply observing how ordinary Japanese people went about their daily business which is obviously an important aspect of the foreigner doing business with them.

As a teacher I learnt most, originally from my students at Osaka Gakuin, especially from the diaries which they used to write for me in English. They gave me a wonderful insight into the lives of young Japanese people, especially what they bought when they went shopping! My assistants, Ms Kiyomi Isoda and Ms Megumi Uebayshi remain unforgettable in their many kindnesses to me in enabling me to understand the students better. Above all I shall never forget their laughter, which used to ring out in the language laboratory as I stumbled over some cross-cultural barrier. Such barriers can be so important and dangerous in business.

Many of my observations occurred commuting on the Osaka–Kobe Hankyu line, a truly fascinating yet not always totally enjoyable experience, but one which enabled me to appreciate the sheer stoicism of the Japanese commuter. Moreover, extended searching for a flat with the kind Mr Katsuya Yanagiya (Head Administrator of the International Centre at the University) at the beginning of my stay gave me a unique insight into Japanese living conditions, also a tribute to national stoicism.

This then is my final acknowledgement: to the Japanese men, women and children who let me observe them and the wonderful lady who, seeing me struggling with the usual load of books, perilously close to dropping them, pressed an enormous carrier bag on me with an invitation to deposit them all inside and keep it! And how could I forget the Narita Airport Customs Officer who at first eyed my bags, bulging with books and papers, with suspicion, but then roared with laughter when I told him, or tried to, that I was a writer: 'Watakushi wa, sakka desu'. Due to my faulty pronunciation, he obviously understood my having said: 'Watakushi wa, sake desu' which means 'I am wine!'

Note

The dictionary spelling of Japanese words (originally in eye-boggling *kanji* or phonetic *kana* script) in English, transcribed in Roman script, ie *romaji*, is not uniform. I have used the most easily legible version for the reader and apologize to any offended Japanese scholars herewith. My sincerest thanks to my teacher, Mrs Sawako Dohta, who so very kindly checked most of the Japanese words and expressions used in the text, as did my student, Miss Kioko Takagi.

Part I

Doing Business in Japan

1

Training for Japan – Preparing for the Unexpected

Is there a key to doing business with the Japanese? Is there a secret to be learned? Is there just one special way of doing it? You are no doubt prompted to ask these questions because you hope that this book might be able to help but perhaps I should state right at the beginning: doing business with the Japanese is by definition doing it their way, that is as they wish but not as they do, because as a foreigner this will be nigh on impossible to achieve. It is also unnecessary to ape or out-Japanese the Japanese; merely respect, certainly not slavishly follow, their business and social culture.

This means everything and nothing, raises as many questions as it answers. But in things Japanese lack of precision can be a virtue. So much is imprecise and purposely so. Getting things straight leads so often to confusion in Japan. Regulations are often deliberately vague to allow case-by-case interpretation. Frameworks are there but that may be all the guidelines there are for individual decisions, which are ultimately based on a feeling for underlying cultural mores.

The Japanese tend not to say what they think but what they can say that will avoid overt offence. The way it is said or in fact unsaid (especially refusing a request) conveys the required message. And this could well occur non-verbally by a slow shaking of the head from side to side and an intake of breath (typically resulting in a sort of sucking noise). The refuser or decliner is literally speechless. So much is therefore intuitive.

So much too is based on group thought and activity – derived from a philosophy different to the go-getting individualistic (possibly 'self-centred') Western approach. It is here that the greatest problem can arise for the uninitiated Westerner impatient of seemingly incomprehensible smiles, even laughter, hiding refusal, while the expressionless face of absolute concentration is indicative of possible agreement.

And then there is the language barrier: a language with three scripts, one Chinese and the other two consisting of what are not really lingual but phonetic signs, with speech differing in meaning according to varying pitch. Above all a language with an extraordinary array of different forms of respect to indicate status or lack of it, with women demonstratively playing a more modest rôle than the men. To the Westerner it is all both incredible and complicated to boot.

The foreigner is forever unravelling, trying to resolve conundrums. The harder he tries to understand some Japanese phenomena, the more incomprehensible they become. Japanese business is one example, doing business in Japan is another.

As a foreigner you are entering a tightly knit world which is often very unfamiliar. Accordingly it is essential to try and learn some cross-cultural basics of everyday life and behaviour.

TIME

Be prepared to change gear, to free-wheel, to accept that your own time schedule is not necessarily everyone else's. Being stressed and in a hurry do not command sympathetic respect as often happens in the West. In Japan it is not possible physically to rush around and still retain the respect of others. You do not obtrude your own personal needs, particularly not your stresses and strains. Not only is it considered discourteous to do so, but it may also be seen as a sign of weakness and be used against you in negotiation. It is better to give the impression of having all the time in the world while showing that you appreciate that the other person may not have. This earns respect and can in turn speed things up, though not always.

It has to be recognized that speed, quick thinking and mental agility as opposed to structured thinking are not necessarily Japanese virtues. This is not to suggest that the Japanese are slow on the uptake, only that they tend to think along established thought patterns. The skill required of the Westerner is to try to identify those patterns or 'mental grooves' which point in the direction you want to go.

The Japanese concept of time is different to that of the West for historical reasons. The measurement of time was, and still is, different. Years are entered on bills and documents according to the reign of the monarch, as opposed to the Gregorian calendar. (*The Daily Yomiuri*, 3 September 1991, page 2, reports of students filing a suit in the Osaka District Court, challenging their middle-school principal's refusal 'to date their graduation certificate according to the Christian calendar'.) The philosophy of time is different too. People may be in a hurry, but they never seem to be rushed. The attitude to time, especially to the key relationship between time and work, is also different. Remember that the Japanese work long hours, take few holidays and therefore have all the time in the world to postpone taking action unless agreed upon in consensus with others. Become impatient with a Japanese and you are lost because you are impatient with the system. He senses this and is resentful because he is part of that system upon which he depends for his job, his daily bread. At best you will then have to spend much time and effort to be forgiven.

This may sound obvious, but try practising being patient in unbelievably absurd situations, especially where you can see a simple Western-type solution to solve a seemingly insoluble and time-consuming problem. Resist the temptation to point out where things are going or have gone wrong unless asked to do so. Or if you do, do so in as self-effacing a manner as possible. Patience in Japan is not just a virtue, it is a necessity. However do not think that there are not ways to cut corners. As elsewhere, there are, but not by challenging directly the person who is holding you or things up. It took me three whole weeks to cash a yen travellers' cheque at a local bank and three months to get a cheque book; and I think that if I had lost my temper once I would still have neither!

It can only be said that the cultural differences are enormous in simple things; forget the complicated ones which are often surprisingly simple to resolve. A general principle often to be observed is: the impossible is easy, the simple impossible. The foreigner has to get used to looking at things 'upside down', never immediately looking for a neat, rational solution to a problem but for what in our eyes may seem an irrational one. My invitation to join the Japanese Communication Association was extended with a notice that informed me that if by a certain date I had not heard to the contrary, I was to consider myself elected; and not that I would be informed when I had been officially elected. There is a logic in this method. It saves on postage and, of course, time.

Time may be saved in one way but wasted in another. The key to saving it for your own convenience is not to inconvenience others, whatever their status may be. However junior a Japanese may be he or she will invariably have the whip hand ultimately because you are the foreigner, probably do not know the language and are therefore in more ways than one helpless. Appearing to be helpless in the first place may of course be the best way to begin negotiations. The Japanese are very careful how they approach each other when they want something from another. Often they will say *sumimasen* (excuse me) to one another however superior the asker may be, especially on the phone. As a foreigner you are asking for a favour, you are a supplicant, not demanding rights, even as a customer, but especially as a foreigner. It pays to be humble; it can well cost you millions if you are aggressive. Never throw your weight around. However, this does not exclude using influence.

Good and comprehensive preparation is therefore essential because Japan and things Japanese are so very often completely different from at home. Nothing, absolutely nothing, can be taken for granted. Certainly when entering foreign markets the Japanese never take things for granted and are the most methodical preparers of all, setting up listening posts and information centres in the territory to be entered. We need to copy them.

The Westerner needs above all to prepare mentally for dealing, at first probably simply coping, with Japan. So much is done 'the other way round' in things large and small. Moreover the problem of distinguishing between illusion and reality can be daunting for the new arrival without a nanny to guide his faltering steps. Do not jump in at the deep end and think you can swim. You will have to be pulled out or drown. This holds for learning to do anything Japanese, not just for doing business, and business is probably the most complicated activity of all because it embraces so many different skills which together comprise the microcosm of the Japanese way of life.

When, for example, you go into a small florist and buy a bunch of flowers, you are not just buying flowers but entering into a special kind of relationship with the seller who is probably the owner, realizes you are a foreigner and thus to be treated in a special way, often embarrassingly generously. Expensive as everything is in Japan, and flowers are no exception (many being imported from abroad), the florist will make them cheaper by presenting you with another bunch of flowers free, as 'service'. This does not only happen with flowers but in cafes and restaurants when you become a regular customer. So much is said about non-tariff barriers and exclusionary practices, but little about this other good side of the coin – 'service'. This custom is known as *omake*.[1]

Business at person-to-person level can also be very opportunistic with some Tokyo taxi drivers late at night cruising around and taking those passengers who bid the most. This is indicated by prospective passengers holding up the number of fingers showing how many times they are prepared to pay more than the official fare. Even treble the normal fare is still cheaper than having to spend the night in a central Tokyo hotel.

GROUP HARMONY

The individual in the West has greater authority than in Japan to obtain what is required without taking into consideration harmony within the group or organization. In Japan, the 'where is the boss/manager to complain to' approach may work initially, but in the long run it is usually self-defeating. There are of course different levels within the lower echelons of Japanese institutions, so that group thought may in fact start higher up than the lowest levels of all. However it remains essential to take into consideration the great differences between how decisions are arrived at in Western and Japanese institutions and how this affects the behaviour of the average Japanese and by extension your own when negotiating with a Japanese organization. The main thing is to antagonize no one, however lowly his position may appear to be and accord no one your exclusive attention because he appears to be the most senior person present. He may be, but not necessarily the one who takes the decisions. Key people may well be lower down in the organization.

Furthermore even very senior and most influential people may be examples of the Japanese tradition of not flaunting wealth and suppressing outward demonstrations of power and influence. As far as class is concerned, Japan, at least officially, prides itself on consisting in the main of the middle classes and eschewing all class consciousness, save according the Imperial Family due respect (although even this is tinged with a certain scepticism, not to say hostility, among some young people and the extreme left-wing).

Summing up so far, it could be said that in Japan, possibly appreciably more than in Western society, there is concern above all else to maintain good personal relations (harmony or *wa*) first and then solving problems later. And no doubt the solution to the problem is often dependent upon preserving a good relationship with the person responsible. That person responsible is not simply an individual but a member and a representative of a group and a system. It is group harmony which has priority. Thus the Japanese concept of time, as an example, is embedded in the philosophy of the system.

You have to prepare to do business with the systems behind the individuals. The best preparation for this is to accept the system. If you are not prepared to try, then Japan is not for you. Time does not belong to the individual but to the group to which the individual belongs. Often what is done during a period of time is, or seems, not to be so important as the time spent doing it. An office worker may stay longer than is necessary at the office to show his solidarity with his fellow workers and loyalty to the company and not just to get on with a particular task. Similarly the interminable faculty meetings at universities have to be attended even though important decisions may well have been taken beforehand. Duty and loyalty are the thing. It is so important to understand the difference between illusion and reality, what is really going on and not what appears to be going on. Facades are important and have a substance of their own but the foreigner should not be taken in by them. You risk disappointment, especially later on when tempted to mistake expressions and behaviour which in the West would be taken as signs of personal friendship but which turn out to be nothing of the sort and merely maintain good business relations. Do not take things at face value. How you prepare for this I am not sure.

It helps to realize how many millions of Japanese are squashed into a space of some 75,541 square kilometres (20 per cent of the total land area which is mainly inhospitable mountains and much of this volcanic). Many Japanese in urban areas live in depressingly tiny, substandard houses and flats: their dogs chained up in meek submission, the washing hung on the lower struts of power pylons. So the whole can only function in a fairly systematized, disciplined way for if it did not, chaos – and surely revolution – would result. Drug consumption is remarkably low, but sometimes it is easy to speculate that the people have been cowed or conned into tolerating such conditions, were it not for the observation that they seem so jovial and thus content, even happy. Is this appearance or reality? The stamina of the people in such a climate is also truly amazing: the heat, humidity, monsoon-like rainy season, typhoons, earthquakes and volcanoes all make for never a dull moment but hardly a comfortable existence. The Japanese have to be tough to survive.

The explanation for how they manage, or rather accept, life so stoically and cheerfully lies in the history of the country. This reveals how modern Japan developed upon lines carefully prescribed from above, especially by the Tokugawa Shoguns who ruled in the Emperor's name and laid down strict rules of social classification and behaviour while keeping Japan isolated from the world and foreign 'liberating' influences.

People did what they were told or suffered what could be the awesome consequences. People were told what to do in minute detail, even prescribing what dress members of different classes should wear and what they should not wear. To this day most school children wear uniform, albeit nineteenth century in style: the boys Prussian cadet, the girls often British-style sailor-type dresses. The sense of discipline within an institution has to be experienced to be believed, even that of a Byzantine private university.

In certain large sections of institutional life, the system is all and the individual nothing or very little. As a foreigner, though privileged, you are even more disadvantaged because you are not truly a member of any Japanese group and seldom, if ever, will be or possibly even want to be. To be a member of a group you have to be prepared to accept a degree of subservience to the system that many from Western democracies might not find acceptable.

I must be the only university lecturer who has written to the President of my Japanese university more than once while on contract; Gary Katzenstein was sacked for seeking an interview with his chairman Morita. (Gary Katzenstein's book,[2] when compared with Morita's own autobiography,[3] gives a completely different view of working for Sony. Both books, especially Morita's should be required reading for anyone trying to understand the cross-cultural contradictions involved in doing business with the Japanese. Both books are honest but contradict each other in the message they give.)

Preparing to do business with the Japanese is therefore preparing to do business not so much with individuals, and groups in general but with *Japanese* groups, in effect with Japan herself, her country and culture that in some important respects is still semi-feudal. Though Japanese people can at times be highly individualistic, when it comes to business a national spirit and group mentality prevail with which the visiting businessman has to come to terms, better still respect even if some of his own self-respect is sacrificed in the process.

LANGUAGE

In Japan once a foreigner, always a foreigner, hence the necessity of having a Japanese go-between, someone in a position of trust, respected by those Japanese with whom you want to do business. Everyone has heard of the Japanese predilection for the go-between but not necessarily why he is so important. He does not so much 'go-between' individuals as between groups. He can resolve problems between groups while preserving mutual group harmony. For the foreigner he can act as a cross-cultural interpreter as well.

In a very real sense every Western would-be businessman in Japan is at a disadvantage because, as a foreigner from a different culture, he may misread unspoken messages and be unaware of being misread. It is a question of tuning into Japanese wavelengths and synchronizing them with your own. It may not be easy. One method worth considering is: try to learn just a smattering of the language. Try lessons backed by cassettes, audio and visual, to get just a little of the sound and feel of the language. A few greetings, expressions of gratitude, apology for having disturbed someone and so on, will help considerably. A few phrases as to where to find a taxi, an English newspaper, even the loo, should be most helpful (see Useful Phrases on p141). Audio-visual cassettes are best because you can see the language, complete with, most importantly, gestures. Often communication is all gesture and non-verbal, or it is the pause between words which is so eloquent. The Japanese are often culturally inhibited from articulating verbally and thus leave communication to silence and gesture. This may speak volumes to another Japanese but merely confuses a foreigner. The fillers, the 'ers' and 'ums' (*etos* and *anos*) are of particular importance. Practise them above all else. Remember too that the Japanese traditionally mistrust orators, highly articulate people. Language is of course essential to communication but the Japanese tend to mistrust it as an indication of sincerity, and it is sincerity which is considered so important.

A wholly different philosophy of language and thus of life is involved. The word-fumbler is not fumbling inside. The slick speaker may be. Therefore take great care to interpret the interpreter. In a sense the language or lack of it *is* the people, so too the Japanese language and suspicion of skill in its use.

It would be ridiculous to expect every reader of this book to become a scholar in Japanese but it would be equally ridiculous to suggest that any time spent in trying to learn it is wasted. Beyond doubt Japanese must be one of the most difficult languages to learn. Even the Japanese have problems with the script. However for the foreign businessman to pick up just a few expressions and to display an interest in the language will certainly pay enormous dividends.

Of course many very successful expatriate old Japan hands never learn to speak the language and yet are very successful businessmen. Others have Japanese spouses and so, in effect, have married the language. One American told me straight out: 'Oh you need to marry a Japanese because of the language!' And he meant it. However I do not want the reader to labour under any misapprehension on this point. It is not necessary to throw everything, Western spouse and family overboard, and marry a Japanese, merely to take the language seriously.

Time spent on the language, regardless of how much or how little you learn, is thus never wasted in helping you to begin to understand the mentality of the Japanese. It is not so much understanding the mentality that is at first so important, but appreciating that it is different, possibly to anything you have experienced before. Again, you can take nothing for granted, and the acceptance of this is the best form of mental preparation. In business relations the Japanese are essentially members and representatives of their company and group. Business, especially at the negotiation stage, is rôle play and ritual and a constant struggle for the foreigner to distinguish between illusion and reality. Once you can grasp this, the rest is easy.

There will of course be the exceptions, but usually ones which only prove the rule. For example, if your Japanese partner has been abroad and understands foreign business mores, this can be a disservice because such welcome behaviour by one or even a few representatives of a Japanese company may not be truly representative. My advice is, in such a situation, always be wary of the one who speaks English well and appears to be so understanding. He may be, but he will not necessarily reflect general opinion and he may himself be the object of certain reservations precisely because of his linguistic ability. He may not be considered still completely loyal to the group and will thus not always be privy to inner councils. (I now make a point of picking out the man who speaks next to no English and bashing away in my poor Japanese.) As long as some form of communication can be kept going, enough to understand the business in hand, then you are much more likely to get what you want, though it may be very exhausting for both parties. The Japanese party will be flattered that you have been so trusting and some kind of relationship will have been built up with the other person. You have become part of his business world. You have got at least a toenail in the door. And it is better than nothing, as every foreigner knows.

Nothing is clear, cut and dried as in the Western way of doing things. This has to affect both your interpretation of events, your responses to them and, most important, how you conduct business in general with the Japanese on the spot, and then how you translate what you have done back to head office and how head office learns to interpret and respond back to you, the person in the field. The whole is a constant process of interpretation and reinterpretation, ripe with the possibility of misunderstanding somewhere along the line. What you want to avoid is wasting time and money on a Japanese venture in the long run. Of course you will never know until the venture has run its course, but you should be able to read the signs of impending failure or success through the years. Above all you should be sufficiently flexible to be able to change course mid-stream. It is very easy to endorse an attitude of 'this-is-the-only-way-to-do-it', and if that fails, call it a day. That assuredly is wrong. Obviously you should keep questioning, taking advice from others, trying out new ways, but if all else fails and long-term determination is not lacking but would appear to promise little relief, then indeed the best bottom-line decision may be to get out before you have lost everything.

THE BOTTOM LINE

Adopting the right psychology is the problem. The general consensus of opinion among foreign companies which have not tried the Japanese market is that it is difficult to enter and hardly worth the hassle. Opinions vary among those which have (obviously according to success or failure). However, among all, it is felt that cultural and *not* commercial problems predominate: language, different customs and so on. The bottom-line question is whether the dollar or pound profit you make in Japan, as opposed to elsewhere in the globe or at home, is worth the undoubted necessary extra effort to earn it in Japan.

Some feel that the effort is worth it because of the educational benefit of seeing how the Japanese do business and applying the lessons learnt in Japan elsewhere, especially, of course, to compete or cooperate with the Japanese outside the country. Others do not find the necessary effort burdensome or after a time significant. A small share of the Japanese market may look a small percentage of the whole but, because the market is so large (123 million people) it means a lot of money and a growth potential often greater than elsewhere. There are few markets of that size concentrated in such a relatively small area.

All the more reason then for the obvious study of the market before you take the plunge and to make sure that the product or service you are offering fit Japanese requirements. Every handbook or manual for doing business in Japan stresses making absolutely certain that the product, service, delivery dates, availability and all other obvious etcetera are of the highest quality. Above all, for a number of reasons, you cannot assume that what sells well at home will sell well in Japan, although the reverse may be true. It is as well to try pilot projects first before committing all your resources. So much is obvious, less so perhaps the realization of how expensive the initial commitment can be.

However all this consideration belongs in the initial period of preparation. Recognizing your own distinctiveness in Japanese eyes is the first basic requirement. The second is to see individual Japanese business partners less as individuals and more as representatives of a distinctive group culture. From these two essentials to understanding how to do, or even consider doing, business with the Japanese flow others:

- As a foreigner, you have to be prepared for a change in status. At one level, such a status can be very elevated. You are treated with every consideration and shown every courtesy. Yet at the more profound level necessary for conducting business, you are not regarded as one of the group. Or, if you are admitted, it is seldom, if ever, to the corps, to the inner councils of the company or organization with which you seek to do business.

- You do not need to speak Japanese to understand the rôle of language in communicating with the Japanese. It is, in any case, a very difficult language to learn because it is so different from Western languages and because of the three different scripts used. But you do not need to know the language to communicate as in many instances essential communication is non-verbal. Meaning is conveyed through gesture, signs and often through pauses in conversation, especially through what is *not* said rather than what is said.

- Going to the top – the boss, the president or whoever you can identify as being above everyone else – is very difficult to do and can be self-defeating. I shall deal later with the phenomenon of 'consensus' in Japanese decision-making, to what extent it is operative or not. The main thing in the mental-preparation stage is to accept that getting decisions from people, agreement and approval can be very time-consuming indeed. Japan is certainly not unique in this respect, but the extent to which decision-making can drag on, may be.

- Even if you manage to locate the person who is likely to initiate decisions in your own particular case, that person is essentially only a member of a group to which he gives obedience and loyalty. Doing business in Japan as a foreigner is rôle-play and ritual. It is most definitely not the Western-type of handshake, let's get down to it, discussion, contract-signing and all set, let's go. Nor is it so for the Japanese themselves, unless they know each other through being in the same group or sharing the same group understanding.

PRACTICAL PREPARATIONS

So far so good as far as the necessary mental preparation and degree of awareness are concerned. Now for the practical side – gathering information on finance and establishing local contacts in Japan. The first organization to consult is JETRO (the Japan External Trade Organization) which is an arm of MITI (Ministry of International Trade and Industry).

JETRO

JETRO not only serves the foreign businessman by providing useful information, but by its very existence proves, at least to some extent, the sincerity of the government's intentions to open up markets. The extent to which the services provided by JETRO facilitate this must remain, in the final analysis, a matter of the user's personal opinion. Does what JETRO advises and says in fact work? The philosophy behind JETRO is obviously not just purely altruistic, boosting imports to keep importers happy, though undoubtedly the psychological element is important. Constant disgruntlement on the part of importers, repeated complaints about this and that barrier engender no little ill-will, and of course take up many people's time to sort out – or evade. Untypically of the Japanese, overworked MITI officials (and they are overworked) are very conscious of the time element, when the time being wasted is their own, though not necessarily when it is someone else's. Bureaucrats are the same the world over in this respect.

However undoubtedly the aim is to satisfy the foreigner, remove sources of misunderstanding about import procedures, tariffs, distribution and other vital matters. If MITI through JETRO can remove at least some of the misunderstandings and thus improve the general climate of trust, then foreign involvement in the domestic economy will flourish and of course other countries will be far more receptive to importing even more Japanese goods. JETRO's original task in the 1930s was to encourage exports, not, as now, imports. But of course its original aim has never changed because the Japanese have understood that exports depend on imports.

The skilful part is of course to maintain the right balance for the Japanese economy. Local interests have to be respected for political reasons. JETRO is not going to boost rice imports and it would be very stupid of anyone to expect it to unless official policy changes. Already there are signs of new thinking on this matter but also of redoubled local opposition on the part of farmers. Agricultural imports are however not just a Japanese problem. The European market is wracked with them. The Japan-bashers tend to see the problem in isolation. This does not mean to say that in isolation they are not right, merely that one should take wider perspectives into consideration too.

JETRO, as an organization and arm of MITI, has a certain momentum of its own. Undoubtedly the very act of having to explain and thus justify import procedures to foreigners, even just translating the terminology (a daunting task) must have led to some rethinking and simplification on its own. Often government departments, even if they have written the regulations themselves, have never had to apply them as end users. There is a difference.

Any foreign businessman in doubt or difficulty, should always consult JETRO and often you can do this without leaving home as JETRO has offices abroad. As a researcher I have the greatest respect for JETRO, particularly for the dedication, candour and sheer knowledge displayed by some members of staff. What is very significant is to see Japanese businesspeople consulting the catalogues of foreign firms wishing to sell to the domestic market. JETRO acts as a purveyor of information to the Japanese as well and thus serves a double function in encouraging the import trade. The impression that JETRO is simply an elaborate cover-up operation for MITI scheming to exclude imports is definitely not an accurate one.

It is so easy for a frustrated importer to conclude that the whole local world is against him whereas, in fact, some powerful competitors may be or there has been a genuine misunderstanding or unfortunate misinformation which is at the root of the problem. As the Japanese keep repeating: 'try, try again' or *ganbatte*!

Finally, one of the greatest boons offered by JETRO to English-speaking foreigners is the general high standard and accuracy of the English in their publications. They are produced with the very greatest of care, attention to detail and clarity – a model for any government publication. Obviously the better informed an importer is the more effective he can be. Certainly JETRO provides the information.

Having praised JETRO to the skies and quite deservedly so, one should not, in the UK, forget the British Office of Trade (Japan Desk) which can provide information and literature. The BOT works closely with the Commercial Section of the British Embassy in Tokyo (the latter is an arm of the former) so that for visiting trade delegations etc from home, much preparatory work can be done by the Embassy on the spot. This is often done through the consulates, such as the Consulate-General in Osaka which is a centre of commerce and industry in itself.

An even closer port of call might be your chamber of commerce, which like the Nottingham Chamber of Commerce, may have organized or is in the act of organizing a delegation of members to Japan.

IMPORT FINANCING AND PROMOTION FACILITIES

Formerly it was difficult for foreign business enterprises to obtain finance locally. The Japanese government has now taken steps to alleviate the problem. Import promotion programmes alone have been increased in the budget from 1.9 billion (US$12 million) in 1989 to 14.5 billion yen (US$91 million) in 1990.

Basically the idea is to provide local and foreign importers, wholesalers and those connected, with low-interest-rate funds to help finance imports through The Export–Import Bank of Japan, The Japan Development Bank, The Small Business Finance Corporation and The People's Finance Corporation. At the same time information centres have been set up at home and abroad to help with promotion. The main point is that now finance is available direct to foreign corporations as well as to Japanese importers, wholesalers and so on. Details are as follows. (Where interest rates are quoted, they are of November 1990.)

- The Export–Import Bank will finance loans for the import of certain products at 7.2 per cent for machinery, medicine and so on and 7.0 per cent for other products, financing up to 70 per cent of the total amount required for a period of over one year and up to ten years with a financing capacity of 125 billion yen. Loans at 7.2 per cent for a maximum of 25 years financing up to 40 per cent of the total amount required with a financing capacity of 71 billion yen are offered to wholesalers and retailers to finance extra services required to promote imports.

- The Japan Development Bank offers loans in the field of high technology, with initial, second and subsequent investments to importers to develop business for a maximum period of 25 years, financing up to 40 per cent of total amount required with a financing capacity of 71 billion yen.

- Regional financing for imports is provided through the Hokkaido/ Tohoku Public Development Loan (7.7 per cent for investments in high-tech business, 7.9 per cent for other imports) for a maximum period of 25 years with a financing capacity of 40 per cent of the total required. This assistance is for imports to the less industrialized regions of the country.

- The Small Business Finance Corporation and The People's Finance Corporation offer loans to eligible small and medium-sized retailers and wholesalers sometimes at even lower rates of interest for different maximum periods and with different financing capacity depending upon the corporation and project.

All interest rates and conditions should be checked with the relevant organization. The best place to do this abroad is at one of the Centers for the Promotion of Direct Investment in Japan, established in April 1990, at overseas offices of The Japan Development Banks in Washington DC, New York, London and Frankfurt. Apart from JETRO, this might be an intending importer's first port of call not only to enquire about finance but to obtain market information, advice with planning and, most importantly, an 'introduction of business connections in Japan'.[4]

Having looked at practicalities, now is perhaps the time to study the kind of society involved.

Notes

1. See Fairbank, E 'Omake' in *Discover Japan*, vol 1, pp96–7. (Previously published as *A Hundred Things Japanese* (1989) The Japan Culture Institute, Kodansha, Tokyo.)
2. Katzenstein, G (1990) *Funny Business: An Outsider's Year in Japan*, Paladin, Grafton Books, London.
3. Morita, A with Reingold, E M and Shimomura, M (1990) *Akio Morita and Sony: Made in Japan*, Fontana, London, 3rd imp.
4. Quoted in JETRO *Information Sheet*, November 1990.

2

Japanese Feudal Society

If you can understand Japanese society, then you can do business with the Japanese. If you cannot, you will not be able to or if so, with far less success than otherwise would have been possible. J C Abegglen (1989) argued in an interview that, in books about Japanese business,

> too much is made of the cultural peculiarities of those things somehow presumed to be unique to Japan and not enough of just straight economic analysis. The Japanese haven't repealed any economic laws. They respond to the same basic macro- and micro-economic laws everyone else does and they are dealing with the same kind of environment. There is too much emphasis on the mystique. Whether it's the mystique of Japan Incorporated or the mystique of harmony.[1]

Professor Abegglen is right. Obviously the Japanese cannot change the laws of supply and demand, but they can affect a foreign businessman's ability to respond to them by protecting local industry against what is considered to be unwanted competition from abroad. You may have the best product in the world, but if you cannot distribute it, it is hopeless. The basic requirement is to persuade the Japanese to want to do business with you. And the act of persuasion is, assuming the right product, often very much a cross-cultural undertaking.

You may be inclined to ask whether Japanese society is classless because there is no, or very little, Western-type 'high society'. It does exist, however, but certainly not to the extent that it does in London, Paris or New York. The whole basis for high society, or for the value system upon which that type of society is based, is lacking. It is tempting sometimes to think that Japanese society is partly pre-Industrial Revolution while at the same time engaged in the so-called 'Japanese Miracle'.

EFFECT OF WORLD WAR II

It is not only that the last war led to the abolition of the aristocracy, and the reduction of the prestige of the monarch or 'Emperor System' as it is referred to locally, but that the whole concept of wealth, material possessions, their display and significance is different to that of Western ways. Buddhism, Confucianism and Shinto as faiths and ways of life eschew wealth for wealth's sake, especially any ostentation. Traditionally the Japanese rulers, the Shoguns (forget the Emperors who reigned but did not rule) insisted that ostentation was to be avoided and there should be no aping the senior classes for which heavy penalties were involved. The present tenets of Japanese management where everyone in a factory, regardless of rank, on occasion wears the same uniform has its roots in Japanese history and culture.

ATTITUDE TO WEALTH

Obviously there is wealth, but it is not displayed to the same extent as it is in the West; certainly not in such a way as to excite envy. Of course there is privilege too, especially in education, but education is available to all as to some extent it always has been. (See Morita [1990] [p 139] on class in the Shogun era and [p 136] on his own family's pre-war wealth in Nagoya as well as his discussion about wealth with Lord Rothschild [pp 135–6]).[2] Moreover, and this is undoubtedly connected to or has influenced religious thought, the transient nature of life in a country plagued by earthquakes and typhoons is there for everyone to see and experience. Japanese architecture reflects such exigencies. Houses were not built with permanence in mind because they might be blown down the next day. Elegant interiors, even in castles and palaces, are muted, ascetic not the least because of the overpowering heat and humidity. Furniture, for many people, is still of stark simplicity. One sleeps on a *futon* (a quilt) on a *tatami* matted floor. In winter, when it can become very cold, the only heating may be from a brazier or quilt over a heated table under which the legs are thrust for warmth. James Rebischung (1973) states that 'somewhat fewer than 25 per cent of all Japanese houses have modern sewage systems, and only about 35 percent of them have private baths'.[3] Obviously with all the modern blocks of flats going up, these figures will have improved since then, but they are still surprising for an industrial country. Exclusive neighbourhoods still have drains that are uncovered; main drainage is now replacing some of this. The extraordinary thing about the absence of so many conveniences, even in the appalling heat, is that everybody seems to thrive on it. People live longer than elsewhere and enjoy better health (infant mortality is the lowest in the world). They do not have GPs either. When ill, you go to a clinic or out-patients. Surgeons run their own small clinic-cum-hospitals even treating cancer patients. In hospital, members of a patient's family are expected to help with some of the work. The whole attitude to life and thus the system is different. The average size of a Japanese dwelling is much smaller than Western equivalents. Traditional dwellings are made of wood and last on average 20 years. Compared to their Western counterparts, life for even fairly senior business executives is spartan to a degree.

LIFESTYLE

While an expatriate can, at a cost, enjoy a very comfortable life isolated from many of the material shortcomings experienced by his or her Japanese colleagues, commuting brings the realities of life back to all with a vengeance.

Travelling in the Tokyo or Osaka rush hour on a suburban train is an unbelievable experience to survive. You have the feeling of being an upright sardine in a tin with no oil, save the sweat trickling down your back from the person pressed close to you – 'touching bottoms' as it is known in the local commuter parlance! And this is no exaggeration. But having said all this, everybody seems happy and content, people laugh interminably so that one is given the impression that life, in spite of its many obvious deprivations, is one long joke. The Japanese seem to have an infinite capacity for taking punishment and thriving on it.

There is a uniformity about Japanese urban areas. It is easy on the suburban trains to get off at the wrong station because the environments resemble each other so much: train station, department stores, small cafes, restaurants, boutiques, enormous amounts of traffic with crowds of people milling in one direction or the other.

Obviously there is the darker side, the really depressed areas which for the Western observer defy description, the desolate areas where the small contracting firms supply the large conglomerates with the exploitation which this can involve.

Discipline

Nothing would work without it. Trains, even buses, would never leave or arrive on time – which they do with remarkable punctuality. At the rush hour there are special white-gloved people, usually students doing part-time jobs, to thrust you gently onto the already crowded train. Officials complete with megaphones, shepherd people into line at ticket offices. There are voices, usually recorded, everywhere on escalators, in lifts, announcing trains, even at ticket barriers, at automatic doors in shops welcoming you in and thanking you on departure. Whistles are being continually blown. Loudspeaker vans patrol announcing what service is being offered and are particularly in evidence at the time of elections. There is a certain regimented charm to the latter occasions, with the white-gloved candidates wearing enormous sashes accompanied by bevies of sashed ladies also wearing gloves frantically waving out of their vans at anyone they can see in the street.

THE SALARYMAN

The uniformity and the discipline seem to fashion the so-called *salaryman*, that is the company employee with the family, the wife and children whom he may never really see most of the week because he leaves the house early and returns late at night after up to two hours commuting from work to home. After work officially ends, and this may be fairly late, he then socializes with his colleagues. The salary-man's life centres round his work rather than his family. For the wife it is the reverse, assuming she does not herself work part-time. The wife is de facto head of the family regulating the family finances, bringing up the children, worrying about their schooling because without a decent education there is no decent job. No sacrifice is too great on the part of the child or its parents. After the first few spoilt years of existence (Japanese children tend to be over-indulged) they go to school and then begin the long grind to university. The grind includes school on Saturday and often nightly attendance at the cram schools (the *juku*).

Family life[4]

In spite of the pressure to encourage the children to work and the sacrifices involved, there is still family life. It may not be in one sense real family life because the father is so often absent, but it is family life all the same because it produces a sense of loyalty in the children which lasts certainly into their university days and one feels for ever. Whatever the shortcomings of a family system subjected to many pressures, as an institution it still seems to survive. At least that is the picture which I get from reading countless student diaries.

It may be of course sheer loneliness which throws students' thoughts back to home but I get the impression that it is more than that, especially when the grandparents or aunts and uncles are ill. The family is not just a family of flesh and blood but also a family which merges with ancestors. There are countless festivals which underline this regardless of the quixotic or ambivalent attitude which the Japanese, often with their two religions each, have towards religion as a dogma to believe in (they do, but I gather, only up to a point).

The rôle of women

The subject cannot be exhausted in a few pages. Here our purpose is to concentrate on their rôle in the economy which would appear at first to be inferior to that of men. Their rôle is in many important respects equal to, if not more significant than, the male contribution considering how much they contribute to the economy in terms of work in offices, shops and of course in the home. For the foreign importer the female customer is indeed crucial not only in her own right but because, managing family finances as she usually does, it is she who decides so often what is bought in the shops everyday.

However, what is their social rôle? Demographically the whole population is getting older and traditionally, as elsewhere, women live longer than men. Also, as elsewhere, they are more numerous than men: five females to every one male. A higher percentage of the older generation of women tends to be married or have been married, if widowed, whereas an increasing number of young woman are postponing marriage and becoming career women. Those that do get married are postponing having children, putting off joining the so-called 'nuclear families'.

Blood lineage

Blood relationship is, as elsewhere, of great importance to the Japanese, and it must be untainted by mixing with undesirable ethnic groups, such as the *burakumin* (village people), or anything which could unduly affect the health of the family. When considering prospective sons or daughters-in-law, a family will go to great lengths to check the other family's records. The melodrama of a prince who fell in love with a *burakumin* beauty, is also well known and a well-rehearsed subject in Japanese literature.

Notwithstanding the significance of blood lineage, adoptions do take place where a family is without a male heir, more especially where the owner of a family business is without one. A son-in-law can be adopted or, where there is no eligible daughter to attract a suitable son-in-law, someone suitable and worthy to bear the family name is adopted all the same. Otherwise adoptions usually do not occur. The practice of adopting orphans or virtually abandoned one-parent children is most unusual in Japan. The procedure for a foreigner to adopt a Japanese orphan is not the less cumbersome for all this. The orphan belongs to the larger family of the whole nation.

Blood however is not always thicker than water as far as helping out poorer relations is concerned unless they live under the same roof. Living under the same roof has great significance no doubt because of the family hierarchy and discipline involved for everyone present. In the home Japan is a matriarchy. The mother-in-law rules the roost when the daughter, as is the custom, lives with her husband under her in-laws' roof. The daughter-in-law is beholden to her mother-in-law whose duty it is to groom her charge for her future position in the family. The mother-in-law can throw her son's wife out of the house, which means disgrace. Ultimately of course, where only one daughter-in-law is present the mother-in-law knows that she will be dependent upon her charge. What she wants is submission that is going to last! The daughter-in-law usually regards it as an honour to look after her mother-in-law in old age. With the building of modern apartment blocks, younger couples live on their own, but often the daughter-in-law is still very much at the beck and call of her mother-in-law.

Education

One of the most important props of the Japanese establishment, society and business, is the education system which furnishes MITI with its élite graduates from the Law Faculty of Tokyo University (*Todai*), approximately 15 graduates a year out of hundreds of applicants. To study law at Todai some thousands have sat for the entrance examination. This is the highest pinnacle of the education system. Like a cathedral there are very high pinnacles somewhat lower down to which graduates from certain prestigious universities aspire to climb in their careers.

Education buttresses the system by inculcating a sense of discipline in the young. Before the Meiji Restoration, the Shoguns were very keen to educate the people not only in basic requirements, such as reading and writing, but also in a proper respect for authority. The Meiji reformers in education maintained this tradition and issued the *Imperial Rescript* which laid down the function of the school and the duties of the pupils. It was considered very important to respect and obey the Emperor in all things. (The former Imperial Flag is still raised every morning in school.) After World War II, the Allies introduced some reforms and omitted to introduce others. However the egalitarian aim of enabling the brightest to get to the top, because it was thought that they would be the most able, was retained and emphasized.

Today the state system is overrun. Private universities, some equally prestigious as the good state ones, many far less so, take up the slack. Some students succeed in gaining entrance to a university only after trying five others and private universities charge hefty entrance exam fees, so they are happy regardless of whether or not those who have paid in fact enter the university. They usually have enough who do.

The universities head the system, followed by the junior colleges which usually provide a two-year course of studies. There is great competition to enter them too. Then come the high schools, middle, elementary, kindergarden and pre-kindergarden. There is great competition to enter those, often private ones, allied to their respective junior colleges or universities because by starting at the bottom of each respective academic ladder, entrance exams to higher up are either waived or assume less importance.

The trouble is that to pass the exams, many pupils find school work instruction inadequate and have to attend *juku* (cram schools) of which they are many, possibly thousands, in Japan and they must be doing a thriving business. Mothers are especially ambitious for their sons, to a limited extent too for their daughters, and do all they can to encourage full attention to studies and homework. The so-called education mamas (*kyoikumama*) hover over their children as they burn the midnight oil sitting over their homework. When you see the hard manual labour required of some workers, you can understand why so many young people want to become salarymen and if possible climb as high as they can in the company hierarchy.

Education at school is often by rote. What teacher says is right. Questions are asked of the pupils and not of the teachers. Foreign language teaching concentrates almost entirely upon reading and writing skills. Pupils do not learn to speak the language so they arrive at university still not being able to do so.

On arrival at university after the so-called 'examination hell',[5] the emphasis is less on study and more on enjoyment. The next burst of activity comes later when students go job-hunting spurred to new energy. Universities have employment departments and counsellors with comprehensive material on the kind of company for which the university usually supplies new graduate employees. The students are delightful and I found them responsive in class and appreciative of efforts to teach them. I have seldom had any complaints but Japanese students are generally not renowned for dedication to their studies. In the natural sciences it is apparently different because of the technical and specialist skills required.

The important point would appear to be that education in Japan may not necessarily be very educational in the Western liberated, questioning, intellectually stimulating sense, but it does cram in a lot of knowledge. There is very little illiteracy. Ability in mathematics is superior to many other countries. As far as the economy is concerned, it would appear that loyalty, hard work at school and stamina in general are inculcated and on the whole this is no doubt a good thing. The impression one gets is of discipline and uniformity. Companies prefer it that way – to receive generalists whom they can then mould according to their own requirements.

The Hondas and Moritas (Sony) were rebels from the system and were the brilliant performers. Japanese education produces excellent salarymen or, possibly as Mme Cresson would say, 'ants', in any event, people who do what they are told, the bedrock of the system.

Food

Food and its provision is a combining and uniform element. Eating is obviously vital to a good life, and in Japan it seems to be a national pastime. If you have the money you can eat out all the time. Innumerable cafes and restaurants are dotted about everywhere under and above ground lending a further air of uniformity to the Japanese suburban and urban landscape.

On TV there are many programmes devoted to cooking the latest delicacies, especially fish. On the trains eating is a way of passing the time and passengers are constantly being plied with offers of snacks (boxed lunch: *bento*), sandwiches, hot coffee, nuts, sweets and cold drinks. Little old men follow with enormous sacks into which formerly famished travellers now suitably refreshed are invited to deposit their trash.

Each railway station has a thriving on-platform supply of self-service packed lunches and refreshments supplemented by noodle kiosks and automatic machines serving coffee, tea and cold drinks, even hot soup abound.

Consensus

Whereas in the West the consumer is to a very great extent king, in Japan his or her freedom is restricted by government and possibly manipulated too by big or even small business.

Traditionally the customer who is prepared to pay the high prices asked for goods and services (there is often little option but to pay) is given good service, even pampered. Complaints are dealt with promptly and generously, sometimes over-generously. But the consumer's ability to break out of the high price restrictions on purchases, especially of the often extortionately high rents and associated fees (key money, estate agents fees, etc) is very limited not only or rather least by the laws of supply and demand but by the government which sets the price levels by fixing the level of subsidies. This is particularly so for rice – the notoriously difficult and now emotionally charged issue between the Japanese and the Americans. In fixing prices, that is subsidies, the government is however acting ostensibly to protect the suppliers and producers (in the case of the rice farmer) for electoral reasons.

THE POLITICAL SCENE

Follow this back further and one comes to the nature of Japanese politics which has the appearance of a democracy but the reality of an oligarchy, feudal in the extreme.

Japanese parties of the right are not political parties in the British sense but more in the American sense, essentially being interest groups strongly business oriented. Those of the left have more ideologies and politicians with creeds and ideals.

The Liberal Democratic Party (LDP) is made up of different factions which unite less out of sympathy for one another than for reasons of expediency. It is they who really run 'Japan Incorporated' and run the country's institutions to further that end. They literally labour under the disadvantage of not being the party of the more numerous junior white-collar and blue-collar workers. They represent the middle classes to which, as mentioned above, most Japanese aspire yet possibly, judging by wages and living conditions, simply do not really belong. The LDP holds the ring by keeping the loyalty of the rural voters, who enjoy disproportionately high voting strength, while not disappointing the urban voters too much. Where the system comes unstuck is of course with the high land prices and consequent house prices and rents.

The workers are kept moderately happy by having work to do. Unemployment is low (officially at 2 per cent though this figure needs to be qualified). Old retirees work too to supplement their modest pensions. The official retiring age is 55. After that lower paid jobs have to be accepted. Nobody starves. Few are opulent. High prices, especially rents and taxes (national tax rates are low for most people, local residence taxes are however considerable for the higher-income groups) together with only a modest range of social services mean that people cannot afford to retire. The work ethic is such that they do not want to. It is a neat phrase but it is true. Many in Japan live to work, rather than work to live.

Extremism and freedom

Politically the extreme right and extreme left certainly do not believe in compromise and are equally frightening. The left let off bombs targeting government and police. The right counter by assassination attempts, mercifully not always successful, against public figures who displease them. They also avenge malpractices in financial houses. In general the extreme right is more powerful than the extreme left in that it is allowed to impinge itself upon the public consciousness more and in so doing appears to have the tacit support of the police and the authorities. Raucous loudspeakers can be heard stationed at a prominent street crossing in downtown Tokyo and other cities blaring away patriotic propaganda.

Undoubtedly the extreme right is able to intimidate the public who, with perhaps the exception of students, tend to refrain from certain political subjects such as the Emperor system or the Emperor himself. Criticism is not invited. There have been some colourful figures on the extreme right such as the writer Yukio Mishima who on 25 November

1970, after failing to rouse members of the Defence Force at the Eastern Army headquarters to rebellion and lead Japan back to its former greatness and 'restore the Emperor', disembowelled himself. A good description of hara-kiri, as it is known, is given in Horsley and Buckley (1990).[6]

All this will hardly affect the foreign businessman but it should make him very cautious about discussing politics or the system (scandals and the rest), even asking leading questions. Japan may give the illusion of being a free society, but the reality can be different. The English language papers are free and reading their editorials (often translated from Japanese originals published in their respective Japanese parent newspapers) can give you the impression there is free speech. There is, but the press has the function of propagating the image of free speech for the benefit of the West.

However in general people are careful what they discuss and how. Good general moral broadsides can be fired off in editorials and that is fine for foreign consumption in the Japanese English press. There is, however, no Japanese equivalent of *Private Eye*, no television satire such as *Spitting Image*. Investigative journalism is sometimes delayed. Foreign reporters complain about being prevented from following up stories. The whole system of journalism is different to the West because of the close, almost family, relationship between reporters and public figures.

RELIGION

Many Japanese who own to have one religion, often have two and, if they are young, will prefer to get married in a Christian church. Liturgical objections seem to be seldom raised to such services being allowed in local Christian, Protestant and Roman Catholic churches. On Sundays the local church parishioners are singularly devoted and families come to spend the whole day in church.

Japanese religious belief would appear to be founded more on superstition than belief and there is an awareness, not evident so much in Western religions, that the whole is to be considered more in the realms of fairy stories and folklore. There are a number of gods in both Buddhism and Shinto, and the status accorded to Jesus is more that of a figure of folklore than the Son of God. Ebisu san is the god or patron of merchants and the Ebisu san festivals are enormous events (which must be very profitable for the temples selling many souvenirs to the faithful who come to be purified by the priests, offering up prayers as at all public events, enjoying all manner of delicious snacks and drinks). One will often see in coffee shops or other businesses, small shrines to a god who it is hoped will bring luck. The gods and spirits are hungry too and little delicacies are left for them as well. At the larger shrines, people often stop to say a prayer. Even old sewing needles have spirits and there is a special festival for them too.

The degree of divinity which the Japanese ascribed to Emperors in the past, including the most recent one, is unclear and probably varied enormously. The apparent liberty of religious belief contrasts sharply with the constraints of social discipline. The ability the Japanese possess to change direction as they did, for example, after the war at their Emperor's command, is extraordinary. This does not mean that they lack constancy, loyalty and devotion. Quite the contrary. They can however change very quickly. To what extent can one apply this to doing business with them?

RACISM

The Japanese are ethnically descended from a number of different races. They are of mongoloid extraction but have mixed with Korean, Chinese and other races.[7] However as a nation they are homogeneous and are hyper-conscious of differences, imagined or otherwise, between themselves and others. Recent derogatory remarks made by the Minister of Justice about blacks called forth loud and sustained protests from Congress in the USA. *The Daily Yomiuri*, 14 August 1991 (p 8), contained a report entitled 'US to probe alleged racism by Japanese Employers', quoting testimonies given before a US congressional panel by employees with Japanese companies alleging racist discriminatory practices in the Californian industry. Apart from the fact that the enquiry was itself seen as a form of 'Japanese-bashing', the wider issue raised was the way Japanese management in the USA tends, or so it is claimed, to exclude local American managers from decision-making.

In Japan itself treatment of other Asians is not as good as of whites. Interestingly enough apart from the fact that Korean guest workers tend to do the labouring, and the hiring and firing process, which used to be in the hands of the *yakuza* (gangsters), has now improved (though could still be improved further), there is local resentment against immigrant labour.

The whole relationship with Korean labour is a troubled one because of Japan's use of forced imported labour during the colonial period 1910–45. Although some of the 145 000 Koreans brought into Japan as forced labour, were repatriated at the end of World War II,[8] the Korean community resulting from this in Japan has always regarded itself as discriminated against. There has been a terrific battle in the courts by those seeking to end the Japanese requirement of fingerprinting aliens which includes the Koreans who have been in the country now for generations. The Japanese Government has now promised to find a solution to this problem more in keeping with the otherwise increasing economic and social integration of Koreans into Japanese society.

It is of course at root a question of education and social position. The educated Korean schoolteacher has fewer problems integrating into Japanese society than the unskilled labourer. The same is true of immigrant labour, the so-called guest worker (*Gastarbeiter*) in Germany.

Where the problem becomes more serious is in crime. The Japanese point to the high percentage of crime committed by foreigners and while they are surprisingly understanding and forgiving in the special courts dealing with foreigners when it comes to handing down sentences on foreigners, they are much less so with Asians.[9]

HOW THE JAPANESE ENJOY THEMSELVES

If you are going to sell to the Japanese, you have to take into consideration what sort of people they are, how they behave, but especially how they enjoy themselves. It is different from the Western, often highly individualistic, approach.

There are of course the hot spring baths at resorts, even the public baths for those who do not have them at home (or it is said in the villages where people prefer to bath and natter in public with friends) and *karaoke* bars where you can sing to the accompaniment of piped or recorded music. At a university gathering to welcome a new professor, we had dinner and afterwards some fairly senior professors threw off their years and to my astonishment began to croon like Frank Sinatra. They have few inhibitions. Likewise at a reception at a conference, some academics performed individual 'acts' or 'numbers' on stage which were excruciating to listen to and unbelievably embarrassing to watch. Yet it was definitely men only. The women watched and tittered.

It is perhaps the man with the yellow flag who shepherds tourists on to trains, planes, off them and leads them on sightseeing tours and excursions who is most symbolic of a desire to follow the leader, to be in a group, and not to have to think about the way. Most Japanese banks have 'nannies' for lost customers, large stores have bevies of information girls. There is always someone there to tell you, someone who knows it. There is consensus, but you need the leader too.

This does not mean to say that the Japanese cannot be individuals, and act as such. When they do, they seem to forget others through inner concentration: the people you see practising their golf shots on station platforms; the train passenger who starts doing exercises to relax his or her neck oblivious to others; even the man who will suddenly stop walking along the road and do leg relaxing exercises. Perhaps, I can add to this the nose pickers I see on the trains, the spitting and loud throat-clearing that goes on.

Then the wonderful ability the Japanese have of being able to fall asleep anywhere, not just in class, especially commuting on trains, even standing up. They seem to learn this as babies, strapped on their mother's back or being carried in her arms. They sleep with such abandon while being carried along the platform.

Japan is the single country I have been to where post office officials are universally polite! My local post office actually xeroxes the odd letter or document for me free of charge and when I deposit money into my savings account, I am given a little packet of paper tissues as a present! I love it. And I suppose I can classify this too as a form of the Japanese enjoying themselves because most of my post office dealings, which often assume the nature of adventures, are accompanied by shrieks of laughter from behind the counter. It must be that the Japanese do not only work hard but enjoy work as well.

It is at the doctor's where extraordinary lengths will be gone to to treat say, a bad back pain, and often to the enjoyment and participation of everyone around. In contrast, at the hairdresser's, absolute silence reigns. It is here that for a considerable sum the hairdresser not only cuts, washes hair and massages scalps but also slaps, thumps and pummels necks and backs.

Thousands of Japanese patronize the *pachinko* parlours (said to be in the main run by Koreans) with their rows of pin-ball machines. They can sit there for hours. Sometimes parents will sit inside while their neglected children rough and tumble in the street outside. The vibrant colours, the loud noise, the staring eyes of the players, sitting in seemingly mesmerized stupor in front of their machines amaze the observer. Are they actually enjoying themselves or are they seeking escape from the treadmill of their lives? Officially gambling is against the law, so they collect their winnings in money from a little window outside! To this the law turns a blind eye.

Sport, of course as elsewhere, is a great source of entertainment viewed as a member of a large roaring crowd or privately at home on television. Baseball and American football are extremely popular among young people. Sumo wrestling attracts audiences of all age groups and both sexes. Most incongruous is to see an interview with the tiny wife of a sumo colossus weighing around 450 kilos. For older generations there are the national varieties of drama: *Noh, Kabuki* and others with the beautiful costumes and attractive stage decorations. Japanese drama is an acquired taste for Westerners, especially the music, the song, and above all the slow, lugubrious form of dance that goes with it. The main female rôle in *kabuki* is played by a man as in Shakespeare's day. Some of the actors portraying female characters are fairly ancient gentlemen, but heavily made up and with beautifully executed mime and feminine mannerisms and these acts are greeted with the ecstatic applause of their audiences. (Homosexuality in Japan is not regarded as being so deviant as in the West.) Again the whole gives the impression of being inimitably Japanese, though there are some Western players who perform *kabuki* too.

Treating the Japanese purely as potential customers, their native aestheticism, delicacy of approach cannot be ignored: with office glue mildly perfumed and flowers (not always plastic ones) in the washrooms; with street hawkers for this or that product, pressing packets of paper tissues upon passers-by. All this against a background of incredible drabness of urban back streets with their sub-standard dwellings. In many ways, they are a deprived people, but with an inherited sense of beauty and refinement, combined with attention to detail, which is all expressed in the products they make as manufacturers and covet as consumers. This is why the Japanese consumer is so fussy about appearance, packaging and quality. It is surely this aesthetic challenge which places so many demands upon the foreign manufacturer.

Much of the Japanese appreciation of beauty becomes very clear when seeing examples of their artistic craftsmanship, be it in dress (the *kimono*), exquisite paper fans, the lacquer work, the porcelain (even simple dishes and bowls for use in the cheapest restaurants can delight the eye), the basket work, the *inro* (small portable medicine boxes) or simple wooden boxes, and especially the woodblock prints which can be bought at very reasonable prices. There is a whole repertoire of native craftsmanship continued to this day.[10] Purely at the visual level you cannot sell to the Japanese and be blind and thus insensitive to their culture. Nothing slipshod and absolutely nothing second-rate will do. A little beauty, a little extra care and attention to detail will surely provide their own reward in customer loyalty. So often it is the marketing gesture which counts – the Japanese are pastmasters at this and thus very difficult to compete with on their own ground.

'Share and share alike'

The Japanese are inveterate buyers despite having one of the highest personal savings records in the world. Students write in their diaries how they spend weekends shopping and the crowds thronging the shopping arcades suggest the same among all age groups. There is great inventiveness and ingenuity in the gadgets, games and labour-saving devices, always eye-catching, a source of wonder and surprise though not all of it is homemade, much being imported from Taiwan, China or South Korea. It is often bizarre bazaar designed to stimulate impulse buying (highly successful) but very little of it is cheap when converted from yen back into a Western currency.

Department stores are jam-packed over weekends, Saturday and Sunday. It seems to be sell, sell, sell; buy, buy, buy. And like everything else in Japan there is ritual and art: the former in the bowing of the neatly uniformed, doll-like escalator and information ladies, the latter in the beautiful wrapping that adorns each purchase if so desired.

Packaging, though often environmentally undesirable, is an important sales requisite. It is the old principle of illusion and reality at work. The wrapping may be much more attractive than the contents. Indeed on one of the many occasions of handing over a present, the wrapping is more important than the contents.

What is important is the act of giving, ritualistic if you will, and value of the object too so that this may be reciprocated. Thus on occasion of birth, marriage and death when money is a suitable gift, a special decorative envelope is given, the exact amount is inscribed on the reverse, and a reciprocal present equal to half the amount is then given to the donor. Even cash contributions are either demanded (charged) or expected from guests attending parties or receptions. The true significance of this is I think 'spread the expense!' We are all in this together; share, share alike. And it is this sort of society you are seeking to enter as a Westerner when you enter their market.

Business and the spirits!

Interestingly enough, Japan, though a highly industrialized and educated society, is still served by foreign missionaries, mainly American. The proselytizing is more muted than before with missionaries no longer seeking to change but to fit in to Japanese society and merely provide spiritual assistance where required. One missionary from Seattle told me that he was aware of a great need in Japan for 'love'. This, he claimed, was the one thing missing. He felt people were only rewarded for their services and not appreciated for themselves. He seemed to be saying that they were exploited. When I asked him what sort of love he had in mind as recompense, he replied that he meant 'Christ'. It would be interesting to know whether Christianity, as opposed to local religions, is possibly unique in emphasizing 'love' as opposed to the veneration of ancestors and the gods. Thus the emphasis in local religion would appear to be placed more on respect rather than love.

The language used between members of a Japanese family tends to emphasize respect: *Otosan* (respected Father), *Okasan* (respected Mother) and it goes down to the children too, the eldest son being referred to as *Oniisan* (respected eldest brother). Of course children refer to their parents as Mama and Papa, but it is hard to imagine Western children calling their parents 'Mr Father' or 'Mrs Mother', though in Victorian times sons would address their fathers with 'Sir' out of respect. Is it that the Japanese do indeed lack some form of intensity or just the expression of love? Or is this just another effect of the institution of arranged marriages which still operates?

With regard to work you stay at your post regardless and get the job done. That is what you are paid for. Not even the industrious *wirtschaftswunder* Germans show such dedication to work as the Japanese do. I shall never forget at the university where I worked, an official being rung up to be told that his wife had just given birth to their child in hospital. It was 3 o'clock in the afternoon. No one rushed out for a bottle of champagne. No one made him even a cup of tea. And I am not really sure anyone congratulated him. I did and then expected him to be allowed to go to the hospital. He still went on working at his desk. I asked the young lady, who was attending to me: 'Isn't he going to go home for the afternoon.' 'No' was the reply and he did not.

If you are going to compete seriously with the Japanese, you cannot ignore the culture. On the one hand it may seem inhuman, to our way of thinking, and yet on the other, amaterialistic. Near my block of flats on 'Nobs' Hill' Shukugawa, between Osaka and Kobe, I have a neighbour with two Rolls–Royces in his garage. I have a nodding acquaintance with the chauffeur. At the top of the hill is a beautifully manicured garden, like a miniature golf course, so fine is the lawn. There is a table and chairs set invitingly for guests to enjoy the beauty and peace of the place. No one ever comes, except a flock of gardeners to tend to the grass, plants and flowers while the birds sing above.

The story of the garden is briefly this: apparently it had been a building site for a magnificent villa. When half-finished, a worker was poisoned, rushed to hospital and died. The building was razed, a priest came and a service was held. Then the garden was built, presumably as a memorial to the one worker who died.

The land must be worth millions if not billions. No doubt it is appreciating in value, though property prices have been falling recently, and the building half-finished and then torn down must have cost millions too. In any case one feels that this could not happen anywhere else in a highly industrialized society, save in Japan.

Every day I go past the garden which looks so inviting. Is it waiting to welcome the restless spirit of the poisoned worker? Would he, as a simple labourer, feel embarrassed by so much attention and the luxury of the garden? Did he have a family, a widow, children?

Of course this story has to be balanced with the undoubted exploitation of workers which goes on in local industry, especially of temporary and even more of temporary immigrant labour. Yet nonetheless, the story of the garden has a meaning for the Japanese approach to business activities. As an American missionary, who was brought up in the country, said to me: 'Foreigners never understand that when doing business with the Japanese, it's the personal relationship, more than the business which counts.' This may be an exaggeration, but I feel that there must be much truth in it.

Notes

1. Interview in Krisher, B (1989) *Japan as we Lived it: Can East and West ever Meet?* Yohan, Tokyo, p99.
2. Morita, A with Reingold, E M and Shimomura, M (1990) *Akio Morita and Sony: Made in Japan*, Fontana, London, 3rd imp.
3. Rebischung, J (1973) *Japan. The Facts of Modern Business and Social Life*, Tuttle, Tokyo, p100.
4. See McArthur, I (1991) 'Low Birth Rate: Traditional Japanese Family Facing Extinction', in *The Daily Yomiuri*, 7 August, p3.
5. Amano, I (1990) *Education and Examination in Modern Japan* (translated by William K and Fukiko Cummings), University of Tokyo Press, Tokyo. Reviewed by Florian Coulmas in *The Japan Times*, 24 September 1990, p13.
6. Horsley, W and Buckley, R (1990) *Nippon New Superpower: Japan Since 1945*, BBC Books, London, pp100–101.
7. 'Japanese people, physical characteristics of' in *Kodansha Encyclopedia of Japan*, (1983) vol 4, pp35–8.
8. Johnson, C (1987) *MITI and the Japanese Miracle*, Tuttle, Tokyo, p179.
9. 'Light-fingered Asians draw heavy punishment' in *The Nikkei Weekly*, week ending 17 August 1991, p19.
10. See Salmon, P (1985) *Japanese Antiques: With a Guide to Shops*. AI Publishers, Tokyo. Gives an excellent insight into Japanese psychology of design and aestheticism. It is also very useful for the bargain hunter.

3

The Japanese Business Scene

SCANDALS UNLIMITED

In the early 1990s it was not possible to open a Japanese newspaper without some senior business or government man apologizing profusely for some malpractice or blatant scandal. Editorials and articles were appropriately scathing as though, it seemed, they were writing for European and American audiences. The Japanese themselves were not as shocked as their newspapers; they had either known or suspected it all the time and confirmation, when it came, was not all that terrible. This may be an unduly cynical view, but I am sure I am not alone in holding it. Bribery and corruption feature prominently in local business life and have done for some years. Lockheed, Recruit, the security houses, you name it, there is nothing new under the Japanese sun. Perhaps only the degree of the newspaper excitement and criticism is new. Do scandals alone make the Japanese business scene? Does the foreign businessman have to bribe his way to success?

To understand the Japanese business scene, it helps to examine the history of business in Japan.

Business in the Tokugawa era (1603–1868) up to the Meiji Restoration and beyond, was always seen as allied to the needs of the economy, and thus the wellbeing of the country as a whole, under the Tokugawas in isolation from the West and under the Meiji desperately trying to catch up with it. Different aims and different 'situational ethics', possibly even more appositely 'institution ethics' are involved. Business in Japan may be 'cut throat' but the throat is not cut because it is communal blood which is shed. Harmony, so sacred to the system, is lost. Companies and businesses get pushed to the wall but not squashed. The Government, that is the responsible Ministry for Trade and Industry (MITI), holds the ring between competing firms to ensure that the domestic market as a whole flourishes.

The most recent scandal (ie Nomura) where security houses

compensated investors for losses on the stock market when the market fell was not really against the law, merely a transgression of a MITI guideline. The illegal part was trying to seek reimbursement for such largesse from the inland revenue. Immoral, apart from the deceit involved, was the fact that only the large and not the small investors were reimbursed. What compounded the scandal was the involvement of the *yakuza* (gangsters) who, like every other organization, have cash which requires investing. It was significant that the only people who did not resign and make public apologies were the *yakuza*!

What is being argued here is that given the Japanese group mentality and community spirit, it was not surprising that a method was found of seeing that no one big was hurt. The position of the smaller business was different, as was the position of foreign companies whose funds were also invested, in the stock market, through Japanese investment houses, and crashed too along with the others. Of course it could be argued that this is a pernicious way of going about it. Bribery and corruption are harmful to any economy – vide Africa. However, unlike Africa and elsewhere where bribery and corruption are rampant, in Japan such behaviour does not bankrupt the economy. In fact one could argue, the reverse is the case. Bribery and corruption elsewhere take place for purely selfish, individual aims. In Japan it often appears institutionalized for common prosperity.

There are of course the public prosecutors who do their job with remarkable skill and dedication, the police who ferret out details and members of the Diet who, with commendable moral outrage, demand complete revelation of the culprits, and so on. Of course there are politicians who are completely innocent of such practices, but they are members of the same system of interlocking networks apparently based on inter-group deals of one kind or another. The structure of Japanese political parties, especially the ruling Liberal Democratic Party (LDP) is group, that is faction, orientated. And the leaders of the factions have their relations with the business world and vice versa. One hand washes the other and undoubtedly one palm greases the other too.

This is most definitely not to express a moral judgement, merely to explain what is going on behind the scenes and latterly it would appear in front of them too. While the topic of business political scandals in Japan is all-absorbing, on its own account worth many books, the primary concern here is to ask whether the practice or rather malpractice is so widespread as to affect the foreign businessmen. Was the Lockheed incident, scandalous as it was, a case of the American company selling its planes with pay-offs to politicians necessary to sell foreign planes to the Japanese? Do foreigners have to bribe their way into Japanese markets? The answer, so I have been informed in interviews with senior British business executives, is 'No'. P H Gee, formerly Senior Principal Surveyor of Lloyd's Register in Japan, said the refreshing thing about working in Japan (after South America) was that there was no question of such untoward business practices. You made your position clear right from the start that bribery was not acceptable and the Japanese respected that and acted accordingly. However other sources I approached explained how personal favours are done to Japanese business partners at a private level, but they are merely the sort of favour that would be done in the West – internships or jobs for colleagues' children, expensive presents or extravagant hospitality given for contracts. The real question being asked here is to what extent such favours, presents or hospitality, give unfair advantage over other competitors who do not or, perhaps most important, cannot afford to do the same.

Given Japanese clannishness, what chance does a foreigner have of obtaining a local contract without greasing palms? The new Kansai airport is the most recent example of alleged reluctance of a Japanese consortium to encourage foreign participation. There have been a number of charges and counter-charges. The American company Westinghouse complained that it was being unfairly excluded from providing equipment. It was countered that locals could do an equally good job. While this saga was in progress other foreign firms were being awarded contracts, notably Royal Insurance and Hawker Sidley. The former company offered the Kansai Consortium a skill and expertise it could not find on the home insurance market and convinced members of this. They then were awarded the contract. Presumably Hawker Sidley were able to do the same.

Obviously in all such questions, it is a very complicated and detailed matter to say, when the foreign bid is rejected in favour of a domestic one, whether in fact award of the contract was conducted fairly or not. It is presumably only when evidence of bribery or other manipulation appears that it can be said definitely that the foreigner was excluded unfairly. And even if he was, it is a further step to prove that for the Japanese a general lack of principle was involved. Someone might have been personally malleable and to blame, not necessarily the whole consortium or what is more important the government. One has to distinguish between personal and corporate responsibility and between corporate and government.

Obviously where large contracts are to be awarded in billions and trillions of yen, national interests cannot be excluded. If a local company can do the job and thereby swell local coffers, then the temptation must be very great to award contracts locally. Presumably this is so all over the world. However there must come a point where the advantage of accepting the foreign bid is so overriding as to make the acceptance of a counter local bid self-defeating. The general impression is that the foreign bid will be accepted, regardless of its being foreign, when it is so good as to be irresistible, such as the case with Royal Insurance. Where however this is not so, the whole matter becomes more complicated.

An important consideration and one that is perhaps often forgotten is the availability of on-site service not only during building, but afterwards. Local firms undoubtedly have the edge on this over foreign companies or if they do not, it is easier to argue in this vein. Moreover there is a distinction to be made between providing manufactured goods and services, the latter, mainly expertise, does not require physical maintenance. Backup can be provided over the telephone from abroad. The distinction between importing goods and importing or providing imported services is one it is always necessary to keep on making and one which leads to another major consideration: to what extent can the imported goods or service be 'Japanized' and thus either be placed under local control or be fitted and constantly adjusted to better fit local requirements? This would appear to be vital to long-term success in Japan.

The foreignness of a good or product may be its greatest selling point, take Coca-Cola or Kentucky Fried Chicken, BMW or Jaguar, but at the same time, long-term success has been assured by either selling out to a Japanese company or virtually allowing the Japanese to run things. Keep the foreign cachet, but use Japanese sales and management techniques. This seems, in most of the available success stories, to be the trick, save where the nature of the goods or service provided requires it to remain completely in foreign hands because otherwise its *raison d'être* would be vitiated. Examples of this would be British investment houses such as Rothschild or Warburg's.

Where what is being provided is more or less unique because it is foreign and that is why it is popular on the Japanese market, then obviously it should remain so. Otherwise the Japanese business scene is essentially very Japanese and the foreigner seeking to join it, should try and adapt himself to it to survive. Again it is a question of recognizing the difference between illusion and reality. Let your concern appear foreign but be in reality Japanese or as Japanese as it can become without losing its essential foreign cachet, skill, expertise or whatever. It is a question of achieving the right blend between the foreign element and the Japanese. If the two are out of balance, disaster will follow. It is this blending mechanism, this almost chemical cross-cultural process which will be dealt with in the following chapters.

If the essence of business is 'managing people' as astute businessman, Alex McGreggor of Cape Town once said, then the essence of doing business with the Japanese is 'managing' the Japanese; or possibly allowing oneself to be managed by them. It is a moot point. How you do manage the Japanese or are successfully managed by them to your own advantage is the real subject of this book which of course highlights the Japanese business scene.

How do you manage the business scenario? What of its structural organization? Like everything else in Japan, it consists of a series of interlocking networks. A foreigner is seldom going to be post-natally connected to the system unless he can find some way to assimilate with it without disturbing and antagonizing it. Call it what you like, you are dealing with an 'Inc', Japan Incorporated (as some writers say) but you do not have to sell your soul to do so, though some may be tempted. What nobody ever seems to mention in connection with Japan is that the scandals, horrific as they are, do get found out; and something, though perhaps not enough, is done about them. To what extent they remain the tip of the iceberg, we cannot say, save that if this is the tip, the berg must be simply enormous.

THE JAPANESE CONSUMER

While it is true to say that the Japanese consumer is very discerning and demanding, it is not true to say that he is so consumer-rights conscious as in the West. Japanese manufacturers provide excellent service and the government is very strict on safety requirements. They have to be to prevent accidents during earthquakes and typhoons: heating appliances have to conform to the strictest of requirements. Equal stringency is applied to the preparation of food and toilet products. Such requirements are very demanding on manufacturers and often cause concern to foreign importers.

In this connection, genuine misunderstandings do occur as well they might do with the specifications and different types of ingredients used in countries and markets located so many thousands of miles apart. The consumer then is well protected but barely heard. There is no Japanese Ralph Nadir. However there are groups which have gone to court against companies whose products polluted the environment and poisoned people. Consumers and environmentalists won their spurs in the aftermath of some tragic happenings. However they still have a long way to go to insist on increasing imports where they the consumer rather than government and local manufacturing interests decide to be generous to foreign importers. Consumers have not as yet found their voice. Whether they ever will is another question.

Undoubtedly the consumer has gone beyond the stage when he can be simply directed or manipulated by government or advertising, though both institutions still have great power to influence consumer decisions through price mechanisms, subventions and taxes.

If you ask an educated Japanese what he as a consumer lacks, then he might well tell you simply leisure and space. The length of his working hours deny him the one, the geographical formation of the country the other. It is really only by going abroad that both are offered the Japanese in full supply. That is undoubtedly one of the reasons why tourism is so popular. Like everything else it is also expensive, especially air travel. As so often in Japan, as a consumer, you feel powerless to influence price. There is always a reason why something is so very expensive. Whether justified or specious it is often difficult to tell without specialist knowledge of the Japanese structure behind the particular goods or service being offered or whether in the final instance the high price is merely a form of rationing available resources which are restricted in supply.

Why it should cost 600 yen (almost £3.00) to effect a transfer via banker's order between two banks is a mystery. Why flights have to be so expensive another. Why travel within Japan has to be so expensive is yet another. Very seldom do you have the feeling you are getting a bargain. Usually it is that you 'pay through the nose' for everything. But then you look closer at the travel industry, say at the private train companies carrying thousands and millions of commuters every day like squashed sardines. Japanese Railways (JR) is the same. One way to reduce the price of tickets would be to sack the many surplus employees who seem to be working for the railways. When it was privatized JR tried to do this but trade-union resistance was very great if not entirely successful. Private railway companies seem the same.

I have never seen such smartly turned out railway officials before in spotless, well-pressed uniforms, white gloves and able to perform military salutes to one another that rival those anywhere else. Many stations also sport newspaper kiosks, bakeries and cafeterias with very moderately priced snacks – the only bargain on the station! There are also, often elderly, platform cleaners who sweep and tend to the plants and flowers that adorn the platforms. On the Osaka–Okayama line they are actually on the trains too, carrying enormous sacks for passengers to place their refuse. Cleaning, sweeping, cleaning they represent a facet of Japanese life which is charming and surely totally uneconomic.

You obviously could run a railway cheaper, but perhaps the resultant misery for the sacked staff outweighs in social terms the value of reducing fares. At least on the railways staff are part of life, part of the throng of humanity, exercising their ageing muscles with rhythmic sweeps of their brushes, members of an army of old men keeping the railways clean. Strange, even amazing, but it is still part of the Japanese business scene, however, uncommercial.

SIMPLE BUSINESS TRANSACTIONS?

It helps when doing business with the Japanese to know how they do business or fail to do business with each other. It is not one big happy family, the members of which simply help each other out. There may be a united front against the foreign interloper, illegal cartels may exclude the foreign bidder obtaining contracts as in the recently reported case of supplying telephone equipment to American bases (see page 47) (with the supreme irony of the Japanese companies colluding within earshot of the Americans!). But in ordinary everyday business where in the West cooperation usually takes place between banks, in Japan simple transactions such as cashing a traveller's cheque involve delays quite alien to us. If banks cannot cooperate at such an elementary level, then they must have problems higher up.

Bank charges for inter-bank services are also extremely high as though banks do not want customers to use the services of other banks. To pay my monthly rent by the equivalent of banker's order, to my landlord at another bank, it would have cost me 600 yen every month. It was only by opening an account at the landlord's bank and arranging for payment this way that I was able to reduce the monthly transfer charge to 60 yen! It subsequently took the intervention of the head office in Osaka to get me a cheque book at this new bank six weeks later. The bank clerk at the branch who dealt with the problem is a very nice man. He just could not conceive that I as a foreigner could possibly need (feel naked without one) or be allowed a cheque book. Now he is forever trying to give me presents, one in particular was a cheque book with designs of Snoopy!

Because inter-bank charges are so high, most people use the post office sending money (including coins) in special envelopes, even to the British Consulate-General which refuses to accept cheques. (Even the mechanics of doing business in Japan can be different: signatures are not generally used on documents but seals (*inkan*) which have to be registered at the local ward office.)

MIXED ECONOMY

Japan has a mixed economy with the state offering 'guidance' to the private sector in the form of directives designed to ensure national prosperity and preserve social harmony. The whole is a delicate, highly sophisticated balancing act, walking a tightrope of economic failure and social strife with, on the economic front, an acute traditional shortage of raw material and latterly labour; and on the social side a chronic shortage of space in the urban areas where, for many people (by Western standards) living in near-slum housing and commuting and working in exceedingly congested conditions is the norm. We call it a 'mixed economy' with the government really interfering as in a socialist economy while at the same time trying to reduce state ownership (nationalized industries have or are being reprivatized eg, Japanese Railways).

STRUCTURE AND ORGANIZATION IN THE PRIVATE SECTOR

The aim in describing the Japanese business scene is to determine how inviting it is for a foreigner to seek entry into domestic markets. The business scene can be viewed horizontally depending upon the particular line of business pursued, or vertically according to degree of self-sufficiency (joint venture or independent, use of local or own distribution network). Obviously there are unlimited variations, impossible to enumerate here, and only a general picture can be provided. Horizontally, an idea of the general span of Japanese commerce and industry is given, vertically, more of an idea of its unique complexity, especially of the interlocking relationships which comprise the organizational and cultural structure of the Japanese business scene as it has evolved until today.

Leading business federations

These are represented by the Keidanren ('a federation of leading industrial organizations'),[1] the Nikkeiren (Japan Federation of Employers' Associations), the Keizai Doyukai (Committee for Economic Development – an élite *zaikai* think-tank), and the Japan Chamber of Commerce and Industry, which used to be the Tokyo Chamber of Commerce founded in 1878.

The sogo shosha

Of the groups representing the private sector the *sogo shosha* (trading conglomerates),[2] formerly the *zaibatsu mous*, predominate. There are nine *sogo shosha* which controlled in 1976 56 per cent of imports and exports, 31 per cent of the gross national product and 20 per cent of 'the total domestic wholesale trade'.[3] One could liken these conglomerates to giant octopuses whose tentacles reach up and down to every branch of trade and industry. They each have a house bank, one of the main ones, and are thus usually able to meet their own financial needs without assistance from outside – though with mammoth projects, especially global ones, this may be desirable or necessary.

They are as follows:

- Mitsubishi
- Mitsui
- C Itoh

	MITSUBISHI	MITSUI	SUMITOMO	FUYO	DKB	SANWA
Financial Services	Mitsubishi Bank Mitsubishi Trust & Banking Meiji Mutual Life Tokio Marine & Fire	Mitsui Taiyo Kobe Bank Mitsui Trust & Banking Mitsui Mutual Life Taisho Marine & Fire	Sumitomo Bank Sumitomo Trust & Banking Sumitomo Life Sumitomo Marine & Fire	Fuji Bank Yasuda Trust & Banking Yasuda Mutual Life Yasuda Fire & Marine	Dai-Ichi Kangyo Bank Asahi Mutual Life Taisei Fire & Marine Fukoku Mutual Life Nissan Fire & Marine Kankaku Securities Orient	Sanwa Bank Toyo Trust & Banking Nippon Life Orix
Computers, Electronics & Electrical Equipment	Mitsubishi Electric	Toshiba	NEC	Oki Electric Industry Yokogawa Electric Hitachi[1]	Fujitsu Fuji Electric Yaskawa Electric Mfg. Nippon Columbia Hitachi[1]	Iwatsu Electric Sharp Nitto Denko Kyocera Hitachi[1]
Cars	Mitsubishi Motors	Toyota Motor[1]		Nissan Motor	Isuzu Motors	Daihatsu Motor
Trading & Retailing	Mitsubishi	Mitsui Mitsukoshi	Sumitomo	Marubeni	C. Itah Nissho Iwai[1] Kanematsu Kawasho Seibu Department Stores	Nissho Iwai[1] Nichimen Iwatani International Takashimaya
Food & Beverages	Kirin Brewery	Nippon Flour Mills		Nisshin Flour Milling Sapporo Breweries Nichirei		Itoham Foods Suntory
Construction	Mitsubishi Construction	Mitsui Construction Sanki Engineering	Sumitomo Construction	Taisei	Shimizu	Toyo Construction Obayashi Sekisui House Zenitaka
Metals	Mitsubishi Steel Mfg. Mitsubishi Materials Mitsubishi Aluminium Mitsubishi Cable Industries	Japan Steel Works Mitsui Mining & Smelting	Sumitomo Metal Industries Sumitomo Metal Mining Sumitomo Electric Industries Sumitomo Light Metal Industries	NKK	Kawasaki Steel Kobe Steel[1] Japan Metals & Chemicals Nippon Light Metal Furukawa Furukawa Electric	Kobe Steel[1] Nakayama Steel Works Hitachi Metals Nisshin Steel Hitachi Cable
Real Estate	Mitsubishi Estate	Mitsui Real Estate Development	Sumitomo Realty & Development	Tokyo Taternono	Tokyo Dome	

SOURCE: DODWELL MARKETING CONSULTANTS

Oil & Coal	Mitsubishi Oil			Tonen	Showa Shell Sekiyu	Cosmo Oil
Rubber & Glass	Asahi Glass	Nippon Sheet Glass			Yokohama Rubber	Toyo Tyre & Rubber
Chemicals	Mitsubishi Kasei Mitsubishi Petrochemical Mitsubishi Gas Chemical Mitsubishi Plastics Industries Mitsubishi Kasei Polytec	Mitsui Toatsu Chemicals Mitsui Petrochemical Industries	Sumitomo Chemical Sumitomo Bakelite	Showa Denko Nippon Oil & Fats Kureha Chemical Industry	Kyowa Hakko Kogyo Denki Kagaku Kogyo Nippon Zeon Asahi Denka Kogyo Sankyo Shiseido Lion	Ube Industries Tokuyama Soda Hitachi Chemical Sekisui Chemical Kansai Paint Tanabe Seiyaku Fujisawa Pharmaceuticals
Fibres & Textiles	Mitsubishi Rayon	Toray Industries		Nisshinbo Industries Toho Rayon	Asahi Chemical Industry	Unitika Teijin
Pulp & Paper	Mitsubishi Paper Mills	Oji Paper		Sanyo-Kokusaku Pulp	Honshu Paper	
Mining & Forestry		Mitsui Mining Hokkaido Colliery & Steamship	Sumitomo Forestry Sumitomo Coal Mining			
Industrial Equipment	Mitsubishi Heavy Industries Mitsubishi Kakoki	Mitsui Engineering & Shipbuilding	Sumitomo Heavy Industries	Kubota Nippon Seiko	Niigata Engineering Iseki Ebara Kawasaki Heavy Industries Ishikawajima-Harima Heavy Industries	NTN Hitachi Zosen Shin Meiwa Industry
Cameras & Optics	Nikon			Canon	Asahi Optical	Hoya
Cement		Onoda Cement	Sumitomo Cement	Nihon Cement	Chichibu Cement	Osaka Cement
Shipping & Transportation	Nippon Yusen Mitsubishi Warehouse & Transportation	Mitsui OSK Lines Mitsui Warehouse	Sumitomo Warehouse	Showa Line Keihin Electric Express Railway Tobu Railway	Kawasaki Kisen Shibusawa Warehouse Nippon Express[1]	Navix Line Hankyu Nippon Express[1]

[1] Companies affiliated with more than one group.

Note: includes only companies represented at monthly council meetings.

Source: Carla Rappaport (1991) 'Why Japan keeps on winning', in *Fortune* (magazine) 15 July 1991: opp p46.

Figure 3.1 The main movers in Japan's biggest business groups

- Marubeni

- Sumitomo (Shoji Kaishi)

- Nisho-Iwai

- Toyomenka Kaisha

- Kanematsu Goshi (Ataka merged with Itoh)

- Nichimen.[4]

Historically the *sogo shosha* originated with the Meiji Restoration when the country modernized itself and the need was seen for an economy lacking in many indigenous raw materials to ensure a constant supply at affordable prices. With the defeat of the Japanese in 1945, the forerunners of the *sogo shosha* the *zaibatsu* groups, for example the great houses of Mitsui and Mitsubishi, were disbanded but they later regrouped and the concept of the *zaibatsu* was retained and indeed strengthened. Whoever from outside wants to do business in Japan, has to consider whether or not to seek cooperation with one of the conglomerates simply because it is very difficult to avoid the tentacles. Figure 3.1 shows the main movers in Japan's biggest business groups. Precisely because they concentrate on trade rather than manufacturing, their assistance can be so vital, or their competition so significant. The Japanese business scene is thus very much their scene. With the large share they have of imports and exports their influence on manufacturing is very considerable. Moreover they also include manufacturing companies in their groups. If, as a prospective importer to Japan, you can establish a relationship with the *sogo shosha*, then things should be much easier. The problem will be to gain entry.

Keiretsu *and imports*

Terminology can be confusing here: the *sogo shosha*, originally the pre-war *zaibatsu*, which Robert C Christopher terms 'holding companies' ((1987) *Second to None: American Companies In Japan*, Tuttle, Tokyo, p258) are essentially today trading conglomerates. However the term *keiretsu*, which Christopher does not quote in his index, but Karel van Wolferen does in his ((1990) *The Enigma of Japanese Power: People and Politics in a Stateless Nation*, Macmillan [Papermac], London) as 'corporate groups', is often used when referring to the *sogo shosha*. I have done this too. There is however a distinction to be made between the *sogo shosha* (holding ie, controlling company) within the group (*keiretsu*) and the group (ie, conglomerate) itself. The one grew out of the other. A great deal of fuss is made about the *keiretsu* because they are so powerful and many tentacled. Undoubtedly they are, but in America and Europe there are conglomerates too, though they may not be so globally comprehensive as the *keiretsu*. Are they a *deus ex machina* or *eminence grise*? Young writes of 'their overwhelming weight in Japan's foreign trade',[5] and explains how they were set up to reduce the dependence of the domestic economy upon foreign business.[6]

With such a large share of the marketplace, it is obvious that they control, to some extent, the level of imports to which by their efforts they can either expand or, by simply decreasing their own imports, reduce. How exclusive are they in relation to foreign imports, especially those competing with their own related products on the domestic market? To what extent can the *sogo shosha* or *keiretsu* influence the imports of others, especially competitors? Robert Z Lawrence argued at a conference recently sponsored by the Japan Centre for Internal Finance and the Institute for International Economics, Washington DC that, as quoted in *The Daily Yomiuri*, 3 May 1991, p9, 'evidence shows that *keiretsu*-type companies tend to be a strong presence in industries where imports are abnormally low', and that 'the evidence shows that *keiretsu* collusion has the effect of keeping tens of billions of dollars worth of imports out of Japan annually'. This assertion was then contradicted, according to the same newspaper report by Japanese government officials saying that 'Lawrence does not properly understand *keiretsu* and does not appreciate the value of these groupings for Japanese industrial efficiency'. To what extent they then inhibit foreign imports is as important to ask as it is difficult to answer. Democrat Senators Carl Levin and Rep Sander Levin, from Michigan, wrote to Vice-President Quayle before his visit to Japan, 19–21 May, complaining that 'Many of the 400 Japanese auto parts firms [that] have set up shop in the United States belong to the same *keiretsu* as the Japanese auto companies that have opened factories here, and there is evidence that the exclusive relationships that characterize *keiretsu* in Japan are being replicated here in the United States' (reported in *The Daily Yomiuri*, 12 May, 1991, p8).

The Commercial Code

For the foreign businessman, the Commercial Code is of considerable importance, even if the contract is not as important as the degree of sincerity behind it. The Commercial Code provides the general framework within which he will be expected to operate. This will have its advantages and disadvantages. The present Commercial Code developed as a mixture of local and Western law and received a new dimension during the occupation post-war, bringing it more in line with American practices relating to shareholder's rights, regulation of unfair business and monopolistic practices, possibly with only limited success but again nonetheless providing a legal foundation on which improvements could be built. We shall see. There are three types of commercial entity:

1. Limited partnership company: YK – Yugen Kaisha
2. Unlimited partnership company: GK – Gomei Kaisha
3. Joint-stock company: KK – Kabushiki Kaisha.

Commercial entities are known as *kaisha*, non-commercial, created by law, *hojin*. Those conducting business (merchants or traders) are *shonin*.

Contracts

While it is always said that contracts in Japan do not have the same validity as in the West, and there is much truth in this, it may be all the foreign businessman has to establish any sort of claim or obtain any kind of regress should things go wrong. The contract does provide at least some common source of reference even if it really only does provide a list of guidelines. Although the Japanese may regard it as such, should it suit them, they will stick to the letter. If not, they will take a more flexible view at the other party's expense. However where the element of mutual trust exists, then this flexibility could work to the advantage of the foreigner too.

All this is or could refer to contractual obligations between local and foreign business partners to a deal. However the contractual relationship, say between a businessman and his bank, is more cut and dried. Where government regulations enter into the contract, there is less or no flexibility as to compliance on the part of both parties. A distinction has been made between the part of the contract which is drawn up to express the wishes of the parties to the contract over which they have the power of decision *and* the commercial framework which has been laid down in the Commercial Code and government regulations to which there must be strict adherence. It is in the latter that the foreign party should seek specialist advice. Always make quite sure that your own concept of the contract is in accordance with local law and of course that a local contract is in its terms not too much at variance with procedure back home, should referral to courts there become necessary. After all, international or global complications could arise.

Lawyers

Japan has very few and wishes to keep it that way. America has possibly a surfeit and does not intend to change. (van Wolferen[7] has recorded that in 1985, there was 1 lawyer per 9 294 people in Japan, as opposed to 1 per 360 (USA), 872 (UK) and 1 486 (West Germany) in 1984). These two polarized views indicate how frustrating it can be to obtain specialist advice and support in Japan. Basically the Japanese have no objection to lawyers having an advisory rôle and understand that with the increasing internationalization and thus complexity of business, this is justified. Where Japanese opinion differs to Western is in a refusal to accord lawyers the right to initiate, and once having initiated, unnecessarily prolong litigation for the lawyer's own fee-generating sake. The Japanese are anxious to ensure that the lawyer does not play a leading rôle in business decisions. The status of the lawyer (*bengoshi*) is not a high one, except no doubt where they can use their skill to reach out-of-court settlements which judges themselves urge. The Japanese attitude is in this respect not unlike the British where going to court on certain issues is as a last resort because of the financial risks involved. In Japan it is not so much the risk as possibly the stigma element which prevails. Moreover there is the view, as stated elsewhere, that even if the weaker party wins in court, the stronger party will take its revenge in some way afterwards and thus nullify any advantage gained. There is thus the incentive for both parties to compromise: the weaker to avoid the ultimate revenge; the stronger to avoid the ignominy, expense and time-consuming procedure of being brought to court.

The Fair Trade Commission (FTC)

The FTC, as its name implies, is a body set up by the government to watch over trade and deal with illegal practices such as price-rigging, known in Japan as *dango*. According to a report in *The Daily Yomiuri* NEC Information Technology Ltd, Kyowa Densetsu Kaisha Ltd and Daimei Telecom Engineering Corp, set up a 'kabuto-kai' *dango* club in March 1981 to win bids for contracts for work at US bases. Apparently the three companies involved were in this way able to win '26 of the 27 projects totalling 18.3 billion yen to install a telecommunications system at seven bases and to operate and maintain a microwave communication system during that period. Only one contract was granted to the US-affiliated firm'. Furthermore, 'the kabuto-kai, which Kyowa said was a friendship club, reportedly collected 0.05 per cent of the contract value from the three companies and used it for parties and golf gatherings'.[8] The FTC levied fines of 275.53 million yen against total contracts worth 18.3 billion yen, approximately 16 per cent of which can be appealed against in a court of law, reduced or even disallowed. Even if paid in full, it is surely unlikely to act as a deterrent to other price-riggers. Indeed it would not be too cynical to imagine the price-riggers at that level must be tempted to include the cost of being found out in the price-rigging price. The point is that once the contract has been awarded and the work done, especially with building or providing telecommunications facilities and service, harm done to other excluded bidders cannot be undone by fines alone however high.

Indeed, it is perhaps a little naïve to imagine that the FTC can ever eliminate price-rigging or whether any save the most draconian measures could even if there were the will to create them. To think differently would be to ignore the strong consensus feeling, nationalism if you will, which pervades economic policy and attitudes implicit and explicit. Anyone competing with local companies for a contract, even if it is, in this case for a foreign institution, is bound to come up against this sort of exclusionary practice unless one can show the Japanese involved that it is to their advantage to admit foreign involvement. I am sure that though price-rigging is termed an illegal practice, it is not truly regarded as such when it comes to excluding foreign competition. Japanese team spirit, the 'we're all in this together' approach, while difficult to overcome is not, of course, exclusive to Japan. However the impression is given that if the Japanese can be convinced that it is in the best interests of whatever operation is involved to allow foreign involvement, then there may be a struggle to fight exclusion, but ultimately there will be none or it will be limited and thus merely face-saving for local interests.

Is it worth the hassle? If it is, then join battle. If no, do not. It is either one or the other. No half measures will work. Nor will complaining alone unless it can be backed up with reciprocal sanctions in the complainer's respective country. But even then, it will rebound in some way. It never really works to force the Japanese to do anything unless persuasion is such that the Japanese see that it is in their own interest in the long run to be amenable. One could of course try and reduce everything to a question of not wanting to lose face, but this would appear to be too crude and superficial. Several faces, or is it masks, are involved. The Japanese never seem to have lost face after the last war. Or if they did, it does not seem to have affected them unduly. The important thing is that in spite of such exclusionary practices, there is still a chance of success. But the existence of such bodies as the FTC alone will not ensure it.

The Office of Trade and Investment Ombudsman (OTO)

This body was set up following a decision made at a Ministerial Conference for Economic Measures on 30 January 1982 to deal with complaints from importers concerning 'inspection procedures, direct investment procedures and other market-access issues'. According to the records a total of 32 complaints were received between 1 January 1988 and 12 June 1989. Of these 27 were processed with import procedure improved in 7 and 'misunderstandings' cleared up in a further 10. It is unclear from the remaining 10 examined what happened, also what happened to the remaining 5 complaints where the processing was not completed. Typical cases quoted by the OTO, dealt mainly with different coding, standard and test procedure in Japan to that elsewhere and their synchronization following complaints being made. The important question here is how fast the OTO can act and whether it has enough teeth to deal with truly conscious exclusionary practices as opposed to discrepancies in foreign and Japanese procedures.

THE COMPANY

The basic large business unit is the company[9] or the corporation.[10]

Obviously there are variations, but Figure 3.2 represents the usual management structure for a large company. The important point to note is that although the structure approximates to the Western model, decisions tend to be confirmed rather than initiated at the top. Consequently the correct method of approach to a Japanese company is not simply to write to the chairman or some senior executive, as one would do in the West, but find a local 'go-between' who can effect an introduction to someone in middle-management who can discuss the matter with his colleagues and then, if agreement is reached, pass the

Chairman	*Kaicho*
President	*Shacho*
Vice-president	*Fuku Shacho*
Senior managing director/ senior executive	*Senmu Torishimariyaku*
Managing director	*Jomu Torishimariyaku*
Director	*Torishimariyaku*
Department head (Manager)	*Bucho*
Deputy general manager deputy department head (sub-department manager)	*Jicho*
Section head/ manager/chief	*Kacho*
Sub-section head/ manager chief	*Kakaricho*
Employee	*Shain*

Note: The word 'dairi', following a title, means assistant, deputy or acting for 'but has not yet attained full rank'.[11]

Figure 3.2 Management structure for a large company

proposal up higher for approval and confirmation. Only after this procedure has been gone through is it usual to pay your respects to the chairman or president. The other way around from top to bottom is going against the system. It could, but probably may not work. General negotiation strategy is discussed in Chapter 1 (pages 6–9). In a sense then, Figure 3.2 is misleading. However, as a foreigner and that is what expatriates are and certainly as a customer, I have found that sometimes complaining, or threatening to complain, to the top works wonders. At other times, I have found it self-defeating. Complaining to the bottom or middle ranks achieves something, but nothing in comparison to a letter addressed to the chairman or managing director. This is where it is essential to take specialist advice.

Relationship with shareholders

The Japanese Stock Market, compared to Western stock markets, is the same and not the same. It seems the same on the floor and, in share dealings, the same off the floor, but underlying the dealings is a completely different system of financing company operations which affects supply and demand for shares quoted on the stock market. Essentially, the shares available for dealing in only represent a small proportion of the shares held in the relevant companies, most of them being held by the companies themselves or in the case of the conglomerates (*keiretsu*), the home bank. Thus though the shares available on the market may fluctuate in price according to the laws of supply and demand, these laws themselves can be influenced at any time by flooding the market to reduce the price or by increasing it by taking up the slack. In other words it is very easy for share prices to be manipulated with control of the shares lying with the companies themselves or with their conglomerate banks; accountability to share-holders is correspondingly limited.

This does not mean that shareholders have no rights or say in what happens, but far less than in the West. However they do have or can have a nuisance value when it comes to holding annual shareholders meetings which the law requires.

COMMERCIAL PRACTICES

The Commercial Code, delineated above, lays down the law. Companies have their own practices which operate like rules of the game in Japan. One of them is the 'Just-In-Time' (JIT) delivery system whereby factories do not hold large supplies of necessary parts but rely on suppliers to deliver them when needed. Split-timing is required. The system has advantages in not tying up capital and space, but it places great pressure on the suppliers and on the infrastructure when, for retail stores, perishables have to be serviced by wholesalers and processors several times a day to satisfy consumer demand. Toyota Motor Corporation is credited with devising or making the JIT system famous and, as reported in *The Daily Yomiuri*,[12] 'using a board with a flow chart of its car manufacturing process, . . . devised the system to minimize stockpiles of auto parts by supplying its plants and subsidiaries with the required parts at the proper time'. The system worked for Toyota until now because its automobile complex and subsidiaries were grouped together in one area, the region of Aichiken. Now however, even Toyota is having difficulties and is re-examining its procedures. It has for example already begun to use Japanese Railways for deliveries instead of road because of delays caused by traffic jams. Indeed it will be interesting to see what relief to the already over-congested road system can be achieved by modifying the JIT system. In any case other automobile concerns which are not so conveniently situated as Toyota must be in greater difficulty and now likely to emulate Toyota.

BEING TAKEN IN?

It is easy in Western terms to see the Japanese Economic (or rather Export) Miracle as one big con for the benefit of big business: American workers in Detroit being put out of business abroad and at home most salarymen living in rabbit hutches. Who can benefit but big business? In Japanese terms it may be regarded slightly differently. What they would ask is big business? Is it Toyota, Toshiba, Honda, in fact the 'big names', or people right at the top of these companies, members of the *Keidanren*, Ministers who receive payoffs, yes even the *yakuza*? If you put it to salarymen: 'Are you being hoodwinked?', I think they would answer no because they are so closely identified with the system of which they are members. Perhaps also, they see no alternative.

At least they have jobs. At least they have a roof over their heads (many people in Asia do not). At least they have savings, salary, enough to eat, run a car, go on holiday, educate the children. What more could they want which they see as being realizable in their own lifetime? Moreover the salarymen regard their work as their existence. They do not want to lose it. Moreover they have been drilled from childhood to work hard, to endure and truly work for their livings. Even during those wonderful university years many will have done part-time jobs, working for long hours, not always in ideal conditions, learning about the realities of life. They know, especially recently, what communism produces. They presumably read that conditions in England and America are not perfect either if your salary or wages are modest. For them it is most definitely not a con.

Moreover when comparisons are made, their company directors and senior managers do not, in comparison with themselves, draw such high wages. In any case if they did, there would be no way of calling them to account as at Western-style shareholders meetings.

In order to understand the Japanese view of their own system we have to look through their eyes. But even then our view is seen through the rose tinted spectacles of the salaryman and not the employee sweating in the subcontract's workshop which to us would appear very nineteenth-century. Does this kind of employee perhaps feel that he is being conned? I suppose, like the salaryman, he is a realist. He sees no alternative. If he could, he would presumably like to be a salaryman too. Yet it could be that his is a family firm. He or his wife could be working at home, where they can look after the children or at least keep an eye on them while they work. There may be any number of reasons why they prefer to work for subcontractors. Of course there are decided disadvantages when there is slack or readjustment in the economy and they are laid off for short or long periods. Then life must be very hard indeed. I certainly would not seek to glamorize their lot. But it could just be that such an employee, especially if he or she can work at home, has just a little more freedom than the salaryman.

Finally, however, when considering present day Japanese living and working conditions, it is surely essential to remember that Japan is in many respects still feudally minded and is pre-industrial revolution or still going through it as are a number of Asian economies. One cannot compare East and West at the same time without taking into consideration the different stages of development they have reached respectively. It may indeed be in the future, perhaps the very near future, that Japanese salarymen and subcontractor employees begin to question the system and the deprivations they endure.

What is repugnant to both Japanese and Western observers is the recently accepted phenomenon of death through overwork, the *karoshi* which is now coming before the courts. The bereaved are awarded compensatory pensions and employees' former companies in their embarrassment and guilt paying compensation too. It is certainly one of the least favourable chapters now being written on Japanese business culture which for all its undoubted achievement in fostering harmony is also based on some massive exploitation of human loyalty.[13]

DISTRIBUTION AND PRICE

Distribution is held to be one of the most difficult problems with which an importer has to contend. It is multi-layered, cumbersome and extremely expensive. However it does succeed in getting the end product to the customer. Or does it? Here an important distinction has to be made between on the one hand the complex nature of the system itself, which perplexes the foreign businessman, and on the other the refusal of a wholesaler to distribute a particular foreign product. Cases of the latter or alleged examples again have to be divided into those where a wholesaler does not want to spoil his relations with other customers or is somehow leant on not to distribute the foreign product; and the sad fact that the product is not likely to meet the requirements of the market for which it is intended. Statistics are sparse. There are many generalizations.

First of all there is not just one, but a variety of distribution systems depending upon the product, whether it is fresh food which requires rapid distribution to be effective at all or whether it is an ordinary manufactured product. It could be a car, or it could be china or a book. Whatever it is, it has its own distribution network or distributors, wholesalers, retailers and sometimes layers in between, each performing a service and each costing something.

Apologists for the system, like Professor Masao Uno of Waseda University, argue that 'distribution costs make up approximately the same percentage of retail prices as in other countries' – approximately 10 per cent with 30 per cent going to the retailer, 40 per cent for production, 20 per cent for marketing. If these figures are correct, and the figures come from the Economic Planning Agency, then 10 per cent does not seem all that much. What however the professor does not concern himself with is the high cost of living. While the percentages may be roughly the same as abroad, the actual amounts are much higher thus making the percentages themselves appear less justified to the consumer. Why is, for example, fruit so extortionately expensive – 150 yen for a pear, a special bargain three for 450 yen. The pears are actually packed separately in little soft plastic cardigan-like egg cosies! Sometimes apples are too. It is a country where grapes are grown but cost from 700 to 1000 yen for 500 grams (1 lb)!

However, there is also the value-added element which is so labour intensive. The grapes one can buy, all beautifully packed, are not meant for everyday consumption but for purchase as presents. Present-giving forms an important part of shopping because of the many different occasions on which presents are given, not only for Christmas and birthdays, but also at the New Year, the Bon Holiday, the many different formal occasions: employers to their employees and even at memorial receptions the bereaved to mourners. Consequently the quality, appearance and packaging of an otherwise everyday food can be of great importance. This is usually labour intensive and therefore expensive.

But even then there is a great attention paid to detail: apples are not just grown in an orchard and picked off the trees, but special foil is placed on the ground under the trees to reflect the rays of the sun onto the underside of the fruit so that the apples look equally ripe all over![14] Again this requires extra labour and care which is reflected in the price. For the consumer simply looking for reasonably priced fruit, ordinary retail outlets sell produce which is surplus to normal requirements and therefore cheaper. It can be the small stallholder who sells his wares spread out on a bench under the railway arch. There are markets which rent out pitches to itinerant salesmen selling all manner of goods, some incredibly cheap and of reasonable quality. But such bargains are of limited supply. Food prices in general are just too high.

There are also a whole host of arguments to justify the wholesaler's margin because in Japan he has so many different services to perform for the retailer who is often short of space and capital and thus relies upon the wholesaler to deliver in small amounts. The question is how productive is the system, as it stands, for the foreign importer? Professor Tajima explains that there are 'complicated affiliations between manufacturers, wholesalers and retailers in Japan [and that] these vertical structures running through many industries often effectively close the market to outsiders.'[15] Furthermore there is 'the close relationship between manufacturers and retailers' to preclude a retailer selling products from elsewhere. This then is the crux of the matter: if a wholesaler will not wholesale, a retailer retail – what does the wretched foreign importer do?

There are the patience, persistence and 'easy does it' people who win through in the end. Somehow they come to terms with the system and take the trouble to 'understand it'. Presumably there are also those in a second group who fail to come to terms with the system and never understand it. They either give up or join the third group of those who bypass the established distribution system and create their own like BMW and Procter & Gamble as well as Coca-Cola. But they are the big boys. Can the little chaps afford to do this? Not all of them can, evidenced by the one in seven failure rate of foreign businesses. Obviously size is significant, probably more so than patience, and it may be that impatience with the system is the best incentive to taking the leap to make your own. But presumably too, there are those who have tried that at vast expense and have failed. Statistics are always sparse on failures, prolific on successes.

DISTRIBUTION AND THE CONSUMER

No doubt the best middle way is to try to enter the system via a joint venture and then, having experience of the system *and* the market, branch out on your own if necessary or desirable. Above all you have to be sure that the product is right for the market. Surely if it is, ultimately the distribution problem will solve itself, which is where the patience and persistence pay dividends.

However the encouraging aspect of the matter is that the very nature of Japanese distribution is changing in response to an increase in imports as well as to the changing nature of the economy as a whole.

Small and medium-sized firms are combining together to make purchases either through their industrial organizations or through such an organization as the Cooperate Import Organization (CIO) Japan. Cooperation enables the small firm to benefit from the cost and time-saving experience and facilities of a support organization. The encouraging thing is that of those wholesalers and retailers surveyed by JETRO, most were engaged in dealing in imports and wanted to become more involved. It is not only the importer who has difficulties with distribution but the distributors with imports. Furthermore it has to be added that not only foreign beginners in the Japanese market have difficulties with distribution, but Japanese beginners too.[16] Those Japanese beginners who then attempt to resolve import problems must then also have their share of headaches. With increasing use of containers, larger combined loads are easier to handle than individual small ones. The CIO not only helps with existing imports but is searching for more on behalf of its members.

A further incentive to increase imports is the changing nature of the consumer market itself: the size of households is shrinking, the number of single households is increasing. Accordingly economy of scale with Mum buying for the whole family in bulk is less and less required; and more quality at the same time, quick and easy to prepare food and other single-household items are. People are becoming more choosy and less price-conscious to save time and trouble. What the consumer wants is above all convenience explicit in the plethora of so called 'convenience stores' in urban areas, open 24 hours a day and selling food, cosmetics, newspapers and fast food. Lawsons is a popular example of this type of store. Whether convenience stores are dependent upon mainly a young clientele is a question surely to be asked in the near future when the Japanese population will become an increasingly aged one. One would have thought more 'meals on wheels' will be required, more home deliveries. But this is just another form of convenience.

The pattern of consumption in Japan is determined largely by a shortage of adequate housing, itself due to the very high price of land. Accordingly the money that would normally be spent on appropriate accommodation is spent on surrogates, cars, travel which includes luxury hotels. More women work. More new products are being produced of which only a few survive. The number of retail outlets is declining, the number of larger ones (department stores) is increasing and will, with the relaxation of controls, increase still further. Shopping malls, arcades in city centres, such as the Yokohama Mycal Honmoku[17], or out of town, including, 'roadside shops', such as Aoki International, specialize in better-quality products not normally sold in such shops but because of their accessibility by car away from downtown, they are increasingly attractive. All this contributes to a high-class kind of suburban sprawl basically taking products to the consumer rather than expecting the consumer to go to the products in the traffic-jammed downtown areas.

Probably what is only really happening is that the general demand is so high and increasing all the time that out of town shopping facilities are merely mopping up the increased and increasing demand. Visit any downtown store or *center gai* over the weekend (including Sunday when shops are open) or a public holiday and you will find everywhere jam-packed with people. It is a seller's dream in one way and a nightmare in another: the buy-hungry consumer always wants something new, something different, is relatively rich and, surely, spoilt. There is a great potential for success and failure in what must be extremely volatile markets but one would have thought of great interest and reward for the foreign importer sensitive to local market requirements.

However it is not only distribution which is changing, but retailling too in response to changing patterns of consumption.

SHOPPING ARCADES AND HOTELS

From the consumer's point of view, the shopping landscape is different in Japanese cities. True there are the large departmental stores, Sogo, Mitsukoshi, Damaru, the railway department stores, Hankyu and Hanshin, but often luxury shops are to be found less in the open streets but in the shopping arcades or the covered so called *center gais* in the cities at street level or spreading out from the railway stations' underground shopping arcades which have the appearance of enormous Aladdin's caves. The reasons for having shopping space underground is shortage of space and the climate above, though the construction costs must be very high. These shopping arcades also serve as underground thoroughfares to avoid crossing the traffic congested streets above. You can walk for miles along these streets underground running parallel to the underground railways. The more luxurious shops are often to be found in the shopping arcades of the 5-star hotels; and the hotels themselves, a significant proportion of them new are, as far as the reception rooms are concerned, opulent to a degree making some of their European sister hotels look shabby by comparison.

The Japanese hotel industry is worth a study on its own, not so much because of the hotel accommodation side which paradoxically is not so impressive in comparison, but because of the utilization of their space available for receptions, conferences and other 'mammoth' events. Alone the size of these hotel conference rooms is gigantic and they are beautifully appointed. The number of staff is also very high and the perfection of deportment amazing. Looking at these hotels, the sheer majesty of them, it is easy to see how great the competition is to enter local markets and foreign companies will be outclassed unless they concentrate on quality and service. It is not too difficult to remember some London hotel where you have been told none too politely to wait for tea because it was a few minutes before 3 o'clock in the afternoon, or the sticky table on which in another London hotel tea was served. In Japan, the service is first class and no one expects a tip. The customer is not a nuisance as so often is the case at home.

This is what we are competing with when we as foreigners try to enter local markets. Many of the waitresses and waiters and bell hops are not professionals but students earning extra pocket money, and by no means are all of them working in luxury hotels but often in little coffee shops for meagre wages.

THE RAILWAYS

The private railways are very cleverly wooing passengers. They provide really excellent department stores and shopping facilities at the city end and in special high-quality shopping arcades. At the other end of the line, they have a smart hotel. Moreover some of the railways maintain their own baseball team, for example the Hanshin Railways with the Hanshin Tigers. However they do not rely on rail traffic alone but also run their own motorways which sometimes run alongside their railway lines. It is another example of the corporate or group approach, spreading the risk with the many different large and small department stores and small shops situated in the railway underground shopping arcades. Concerts are held in the Japan Railway main terminus in Tokyo, which has such an attractive Meiji façade. The Japanese never seem to waste space be it for business or culture.

SUPERMARKET TASTES

Difference in consumer taste was well described by Koyo Yamada of The Daiei Inc, in a lecture at a JETRO Seminar held in October 1988. He enunciated his message to prospective employers very clearly: 'you must follow what Japanese people are used to'[18] and this often means appearance. Labelling on tins is very important, restrained colours and the text in Japanese, better printed rather than paper labelled cans. It is not necessarily an advantage to advertise that the product is imported ('imports should blend more easily onto store shelves in Japan,' Yamada added). Size is important too. Japanese customers have little room at home, like to buy fresh food frequently and so do not need large quantities, but prefer small ones. The example he gave was of tea bags, packages of 25 sell better than of 100. Daiei also likes extra refinements on clothing sold in their stores, proper metal buttons rather than plastic or shell ones.

Daiei demands quality for its customers but, one has to add, their shops are not prestigiously appointed. However I have found Daiei sells good quality at very reasonable prices, especially in simple furniture which elsewhere is extremely expensive. Daiei also has bargains in electrical goods, washing machines, vacuum cleaners and refrigerators. It also provides good after-sales service for the general run of goods it sells. it also provides its own guarantee which can be more generous than that of the manufacturer. Anyone setting up a household on a relative shoestring in Japan should make a bee-line for Daiei. Its china and glassware is very good, some of it British. I have found its staff also very helpful.

Daiei works on the same system as the UK's Marks & Spencer in maintaining close links with manufacturers and where complaints occur, visiting the factory concerned and getting to the root of the problem, if need be offering advice on its rectification. Daiei also has its own system of testing goods sold in its stores. Indeed Daiei and Marks & Spencer have done business together in the past. What Japan needs is a Boots the Chemist and possibly a W H Smiths.

The great problem seems to be space, even in the large stores. Over weekends there just is not the room to move about in comfort. However this is a problem everywhere. And that is the great tragedy of Japan. The Japanese can buy and have everything, except space. Not even the richest of the rich seem to have much of it. Probably the Emperor is the only person to have a really large garden which he very graciously shares with his subjects who are allowed to visit the Imperial Palace Gardens in Tokyo most days of the year. The only problem with Daiei is that it must put all the smaller shops out of business which are more expensive but are so much part of the urban scene. However, Daiei encourages the small man too in leasing out space for individual shops within their store. With the coming simplification of regulations regarding the entry of large American retailers, the pressure on the small shopkeeper will be even more severe.

Notes

1. van Wolferen, K (1990) *The Enigma of Japanese Power*, Macmillan (Papermac), London, p45.
2. Young, A K (1989) *The Sogo Shosha. Japan's Multinational Trading Companies*, Tuttle, Tokyo.
3. ibid, pxix.
4. ibid, pp11–13.
5. ibid, p13.
6. ibid, p24.
7. van Wolferen, K (1990) *The Enigma of Japanese Power*, Macmillan (Papermac), London, p281, p602, fn40.

8. See (1991) 'US targets keiretsu issue in SII talks' report in *The Daily Yomiuri*, 9 May, p9.
9. Clark, R (1988) *The Japanese Company*, Tuttle, Tokyo.
10. Lu, D J (1989) *Inside Corporate Japan: The Art of Fumble-Free Management*, Tuttle, Tokyo.
11. See (1988) 'Principal Positions in a Typical Japanese Firm' in *Doing Business in Japan*, JETRO Marketing Series 8, revised 1988: p14.
12. *The Daily Yomiuri* (1991) '"Just-In-Time" delivery sits at the crossroads', 12 May, p8.
13. See Kawahito Hiroshi 'Death and the Corporate Warrior', in *Japan Quarterly* (April–June) pp149–57; and National Defense Counsel for Victims of Karoshi (1990) *KAROSHI: When the 'Corporate Warrior' dies*, Tokyo.
14. For information on this point, I am indebted to Dennis Grass of Ado Electronic Industrial Co, Ltd, Osaka, who gave me a detailed and most sensitive description of the often labour-intensive, value-added concept which applies to the preparation and marketing of Japanese products. The high price is sometimes regarded by the customer as an asset when making the purchase – see p73.
15. Tajima, Y (1991) 'Japanese market holds promise for foreign manufacturers' in *A Wealth of Opportunity: Distribution in Japan*, JETRO, Tokyo, p43.
16. Ibid (under heading 'Impediments also hurt Japanese firms'), p43.
17. JETRO, March 1991, 'Honmoku Marks New Era in Shopping Centres' in *A Wealth of Opportunity: Distribution in Japan*, pp24–6.
18. ibid, p27.

4

Trying to Enter the Market

The quickest entry you might think is to take over a local company. Try this and you soon learn that 'Japan is not for sale!' because that is how it is regarded. And understanding this makes the whole problem of tariff and non-tariff barriers easier to comprehend. Business to a Japanese is not just profit but something more. The local anti-takeover syndrome is an important example.

TAKEOVER RESISTANCE

One of the greatest barriers to foreign entry to the Japanese market is resistance to foreign takeover of Japanese companies. The Japanese take over foreign companies with abandon, as much as 25 per cent of Californian banking, Hollywood's Columbia Corporation, but when the Americans try to do the same, they are frustrated. The Japanese argue that personnel often suffer, people lose their jobs, asset-stripping occurs as in the USA, the whole is regarded purely as an economic and not as a human exercise.

Undoubtedly there is much in this but it is felt that the real, underlying reason is a built-in psychological resistance to foreign control. Such resistance is not only in the business domain but elsewhere. Indeed foreigners are rarely allowed to be on the board of Japanese organizations per se and there is even resistance to foreigners having chairs at some universities. There does seem to be definite resistance to foreigners being allowed to exert a controlling influence, although advisory is admissible, in Japanese organizations.

The foreigner is regarded as a guest. Control must seem to the Japanese mind reminiscent of colonialism and surely in a sense they are right. In the past some large American companies, such as the United Fruit Company, used virtually to rule some South American countries and Japan knows that if it really came to a takeover power struggle, deficit or no deficit, America would have the resources to outbid the

Japanese, were the effort to be made. America Inc could outbid Japan Inc. Japan is therefore only willing to allow limited penetration of its markets. It will always resist an outright takeover.

At the end of the last war defeat was complete, humiliation absolute. America, if so disposed, could have taken over the country, possibly made it into a second Philippines, with, who knows, better or worse results. Japan saw its opportunity in keeping its freedom by copying the Americans, but was always determined not to be swallowed up by them. Indeed now it is they who are swallowing the Americans.

In a very real, however hidden, way the last war has never ended, certainly neither ministerially or bureaucratically. Chalmers Johnson tells the whole story, which reads like a saga, in his excellent book *MITI and The Japanese Miracle. The Growth of Industrial Policy, 1925–1975*.[1] He shows how the Japanese Government, which economically speaking, had got so many things wrong before and during the last war, was determined to get them right in the future. With the policy of 'administrative guidance', they did; basically by rationalizing the host of smaller firms, supporting the vital export industries which they changed from agricultural and textiles to automobiles and electronics, providing protection against foreign competition at home with high domestic prices to subsidize cheap exports, while at the same time relentlessly obtaining foreign expertise from foreign importers whom they only allowed to import on government-dictated terms.

Johnson pays tribute to all the other necessary Japanese qualities of promoting harmony, company loyalty, compliant unions, job security, work ethic and of course the system of bank-based manufacturing conglomerates, high loaning for industry, *keiretsu* supply conglomerates for obtaining raw materials, mini welfare-state facilities, modest living conditions, and so on. But is adamant that MITI (the Ministry of Trade and Industry) was, and to a very great extent still is, the real hero. The Japanese 'economic miracle' was the result of combined national and nationalistic effort led and supervised from above. Government-inspired capitalism with 'the ugly face' removed but without socialist pampering either. Possibly only the Japanese could have conceived it and only the Japanese could have put up with it. They did and have now become world-beaters.

Johnson's thesis is a most convincing one. Possibly, however, it does not pay sufficient attention to the sheer quality of Japanese industrialists, especially the iconoclastic mavericks such as Sony's Akio Morita or Honda's Soichiro Honda. But the sheer weight of Johnson's scholarship and direct observations of the obedient nature of the Japanese to government and direction from above, make the whole story, which is still continuing, credible. The struggle, the 'war' is still waged.[2]

IS ENTRY POSSIBLE?

Can you get into the market at all, let alone 'enter' it with all those barriers you have read about? It is certainly the most important and difficult question to answer because all depends, as the Japanese say, 'case by case' and on your own determination. If you are bent on importing rice, then obviously you will need considerable determination, though things are beginning to change due to intense American pressure on this issue. If you wanted to import certain types of leather goods, there might be problems too. Officially Japan has scrapped or drastically reduced many tariffs and has fewer than other countries. It is really the non-tariff barriers which can be so unexpected and trying and they may be case by case, seemingly at first without rhyme or reason or just plain unreasonable.

Where they do occur, there are various procedures which can be followed to alleviate or even remove them officially, but the time, trouble and sheer expense of so doing may outweigh the amount of time and capital you are prepared to invest. It could of course be that the best-researched project suddenly flounders because of local opposition from a prospective competitor who feels threatened and really is not prepared to tolerate competition. It should not be too difficult to find out who it is. Whether you can come to some agreement with the reluctant competitor is a matter for negotiation, and it is advisable to consult JETRO (or even MITI) who may be able to help, certainly to advise.

If this proves ineffective, then consider partnership with a local joint venturer who may be powerful enough to remove or reduce the non-tariff barriers. If all else fails, then seek assistance from your own government. It really then is a question of deciding how much you are prepared to invest in overcoming difficulties. Some simply resort to bribery and get caught. (Presumably there are those who succeed but apart from the moral dimension the risk of being discovered does not in the long run make it worthwhile.) The Lockheed Scandal is the supreme example of very high stakes indeed and where presumably the risks involved were considered and grossly miscalculated. The harm done psychologically to Japan's reputation and, of course, to the perpetrators was so immense because it suggested that not only does every man have his price but also every country.

Japan may be one of the most successful economies in the world and probably is, but that said, it is still a late starter and is thus caught between the old and the new. Sudden wealth brings its own problems both for countries and individuals, for Japan just as it does for those in the City of London, New York or Chicago. Nakasone or Ivan Bowsky are figures symptomatic of temptations and responses that can arise everywhere, appal and frighten us in the Old and New Worlds, East and West.

DIRECT FOREIGN INVESTMENT IN JAPAN

Whatever the difficulties of doing business in Japan, the number of non-tariff barriers and problems with the distribution system encountered, statistics compiled by JETRO show that foreign investment in Japan is increasing 'dramatically',[3] doubling from US$1.5 billion (1976–80) to US$3.3 billion (1981–5). The USA heads the list with over 50 per cent of total investment, Switzerland is in second place, followed by the UK and West Germany (prior to reunification). The European countries provide 20 per cent of direct investment. Although manufacturing accounts for 68.6 per cent of direct foreign investment and machinery and chemical industries have 25.7 per cent and 22.6 per cent shares of foreign investment respectively, the general movement is away 'from machine tools to electronics in the machinery industry, and from petrochemicals to fine chemicals in the chemical industry'.[4] This, according to the JETRO survey, reflects the move 'away from "solid and large scale" to "light and small scale" in the course of Japan's becoming a more high-tech-oriented industrial society'.[5] The survey also revealed that return on money, 'the ratio of ordinary profit to net sales',[6] was higher than that obtained by Japanese companies. Apparently in the electric equipment industry, this was 'three times higher than that of the average for all Japanese corporations'.[7] To what extent this is connected with different accounting practices was not discussed – see page 77 – and one naturally has to be very careful about interpreting statistics. However it would appear that direct foreign investment pays off quite handsomely with, in 1987, over 6 per cent average returns for all foreign companies surveyed and 6.9 per cent for those in the manufacturing industry being recorded.

SALES TECHNIQUE

How are you going to do business with the Japanese, sell to them? You read the preface to this book, perhaps glance through Chapter 1 and then, after consulting the list of contents, either go for a subject which catches your attention or conscientiously go through from first to last chapter. You might well keep asking yourself: 'Yes, but when's he getting to the point? When's he going to tell me how I do business with the Japanese, sell them something? Why doesn't he get down to it?' Yawn, glance at watch, put book down in disgust.

Please do not do that! It is not really you doing business with the Japanese so much as their doing it with you. You will often find in relations with the Japanese, that you think you are in charge or the initiator, but this is only illusion, the reality is different: they are in charge. You can offer them this or that, do what you like, but the final act is up to them. It is they, the customer or client, who decides (as elsewhere) but more so in Japan because you are on their territory, almost their prisoner. They usually have so much choice. They do not need to buy, but you need to sell and they know it. It is not just the purely business side which is at issue but the foreign national. This is why you have to judge and test your own effectiveness in selling to the Japanese. If you have difficulties selling directly, do it indirectly through a local agent or employ local sales staff.

I am sure the degree of personal involvement in selling is important. Obviously in a large concern others do the job for you or can if you let them. Yet it may be that your company's greatest sales asset is you after all. Japanese like personal attention. They will get details from your staff, but they like to know you, the boss, or one of the bosses, are interested. This proves sincerity. This sells. Proven and visible care and dedication are of paramount importance.

It is so obvious, but precisely because of this it is often forgotten. Remote impersonal control does not work in Japan. British aloofness (now an old-fashioned stereotype one hopes?) and American brashness (surely also?) do not help either. It has to be the right Japanese social mix.

COMPETITION – POSSIBLY DON'T!

The great problem when attempting doing business with the Japanese is the question of exclusionary practices. Doing business with the Japanese does not usually present a problem unless one has to compete with them. Japanese culture is a group culture of interlocking relationships. It is so structured that everyone holds together when threatened from outside. You do not want to be that threat. Competition between Japanese does exist and it can be as cut-throat as elsewhere, but when faced with competition from without, old internal rivalries tend to be forgotten.

Those foreign expatriate businessmen who tell you anyone can do business in Japan invariably do not compete with the locals. The last thing you should try and do is compete save with other foreigners, which is often what expatriate firms spend most of their time doing – competing against each other for the market in Japan. However compete with the Japanese, and you are asking for trouble.

Why? A foreigner is more or less welcome in Japan. However, he has never been welcome as a challenger, even and especially in sumo wrestling, or baseball or as a questioner of established ideas and customs. He is certainly not welcomed as a competitor in trade and industry. He is only welcome when he can fill gaps and needs which locals cannot fill.

It is no use claiming, as Americans do, that this is unfair because they are not so exclusionary-minded back home. Even assuming that this is always the case, and it is not always so, then it should be remembered that the US was built on different ideals: its very raison d'être was to welcome foreign ideas. There was room for all, so many gaps to fill. Now in the USA anti-Japanese feeling runs high. The Japanese have always been exclusionists and isolationists. Probably they will always be so. Only those Japanese who have studied and worked abroad and are thus accustomed to free international competition on a country's home ground, will understand, but then when they return to Japan, they often feel ostracized by their own people.

Japanese reluctance to admit the foreign competitor will not prevent them from competing with the foreigner by trying to produce a cheaper or possibly a better product if they can. Witness the Procter and Gamble nappies ('diapers' as the Americans call them) war with Procter and Gamble first establishing a market, filling a gap, a Japanese company producing a cheaper substitute and Procter and Gamble ultimately after a period of drastically falling sales making a comeback with an improved product that did not really compete with the local version. After all it was a battle for Japanese babies' bottoms and not for American ones. Competition on the Japanese home market is for Japanese and for foreigners among their respective selves alone, if harmony is to prevail.

The best tactic is therefore to try and de-internationalize competition by combining with a Japanese partner. Go it alone, and you will come up against those non-tariff barriers. You will get caught in the tentacles. You can choose any analogy you like, probably the spider's web is the most appropriate – and you are the fly. You will get stuck, smothered and eaten!

Obviously there are going to be exceptions and we shall be dealing with some when examining a survey of a number of successful foreign companies in Japan conducted by JETRO. Here we are only considering the general problem of entering the market and avoiding competition.

FINDING A LOCAL PARTNER

To what extent should the whole be a joint or an independent venture? Obviously this depends on the nature of the product or service to be offered and presumably also on the degree of market research which has hopefully gone before.

The joint-venture approach offers the advantage of leaving much of the Japanese side of things to the Japanese partner, who is presumably better able than the foreigner, in the case of imports, to deal with local formalities and so on. However, great care must obviously be taken on choice of partner because, once the wedding has taken place, divorce could be a very expensive and messy business. Word soon gets round and finding a second partner may be correspondingly more difficult.

There is a science involved in finding the right sort of venture partner and great care must be exercised to ensure that the partner is not just interested in obtaining expertise to use and market himself at a later date. Trust is involved and great care must be taken in whom one reposes it. This is where previous research is so vital and JETRO is a good place to start off with. Their services are comprehensive and have full government backing. Banks oblige too for obvious reasons. But whatever precautions one takes and however well prepared, any choice of venture partner involves risk, but even this may prove less risky than going it alone. (Going it alone obviously requires considerably more research and most probably capital investment too. Simply – and this is by no means simple – setting up an office in Tokyo is a costly business, more so than anywhere else in the world. However sharing office services is more sensible to begin with, should funds be limited, until you have got a foothold.)

There are a number of local consultants (Japanese and expatriate) who offer liaison services, database information, the lot. How effective they are is another matter. I am always wary of those who do not speak Japanese fluently. I feel they are probably more effective in reverse, helping Japanese businessmen to access foreign markets.

IGNORANCE, THE GREATEST NON-TARIFF BARRIER

The greatest non-tariff barrier to importing into Japan is, according to Barry Rosenstock, director of the State of Ohio Department of Development in Tokyo and president of the American State Offices Association, 'Ignorance'. He gives as an example someone from Ohio wanting to export a special kind of plastic product to Japan. The idea seems great to the would-be exporter who then has to find a Japanese importer interested in the product. This requires discovering who in Japan can use this type of product. Apparently there are no trade directories in English which will list this type of information.

The only way to find the information is to know someone in Japan who knows the person the Ohio manufacturer is looking for. Not even JETRO can help, although that organization has compiled a comprehensive directory of local traders in every branch of industry and commerce.[8]

Isolated as this particular example may be, there are no doubt others. Of course the volume and value of such trade may be small, but every export and import has its potential multiplier: one thing can lead to another. Government departments have obviously got a lot of fact-finding to do. Again language is an important part of the problem in exchanging vital grass-roots information.

However even if one were able to locate the potential Japanese importer, this does not necessarily mean that any transaction would occur. Even if the Japanese, once contacted, were interested, he might well balk at the extra administrative, especially the linguistic effort involved. Establishing contact might not be enough. Some support, especially translation services might be necessary. (And they would not be cheap.)

One wonders to what extent already trade organizations within different countries interested in increasing exports to Japan are always in contact enough with their Japanese opposite numbers. Or could it be that language again is the problem, at least to some extent? Perhaps too funds are limited for such work. There are so many 'ifs and buts', but there is still much work to be done in the information field. The ultimate aim has surely got to be that any potential exporter has to be able to locate his or her Japanese number as quickly and as easily as possible and be provided with some degree of support if necessary.

The problem is not just a commercial but a social one of bringing the exporter and importer together as people. Japan is so far away which makes the problem more intractable for some. Yet the twinning of cities, youth-exchange programmes, indeed any form of international exchange at human level, must help. History does not help and Japan is still very isolationist in many respects. Yet there is a genuine desire on the part of many Japanese to learn about foreign countries and visit them. Surely this desire should be reciprocated. You cannot want to export to a foreign country in the abstract, devoid of the human element.

MECHANICS OF OPENING A REPRESENTATIVE OFFICE IN JAPAN

This is only a rough and not a comprehensive guide. Let us assume that you have both a passport and visa, either short term for up to 90 days or a posting visa with residence status up to three years and a specified visa for the same length of time for the family. The local Japanese consulate will arrange this. Above all remember that if you are going to go backwards and forwards to and from Japan, you need a re-entry permit otherwise you have to surrender your alien registration (ID) card which you have to apply for within 90 days of arrival from the local ward office (town hall). Please remember: the visa for initial entry and permission to stay is one thing, permission to leave and re-enter the country within the duration of your visa's validity, is another. Be prepared to have your fingerprints taken. There is no way round this.

On arrival, you will want to find office space. Either do this through a private foreign company such as Helpmates (see page 110) or the Jardine Business Centre (see page 110) or through a Japanese estate office. Good estate agents will help you with other aspects of settling in. Or you can try and find office space advertised in the English-language press. It all depends how quickly you want to find somewhere and how much you are prepared to pay.

Obviously much preparatory work could be done by mail, fax and telephone before arrival, at least so that you can go to see places immediately rather than waste valuable time making preliminary enquiries from an expensive hotel room. Assuming you will want to open an office in Tokyo first, then normally, depending upon your line of business, your choice of location will be restricted to the city centre, expensive but conveniently accessible for you and your prospective clients. Whether or not to take your family will depend upon the intended length of your stay. It might be better to find accommodation first before the family follows: the search for private accommodation, unless your funds are unlimited, can be long and tedious.

Alternately you might be tempted to try combining the office with accommodation, but would probably not be able to afford living accommodation in the centre of town or an office out of town in affordable living accommodation which would be very convenient for conducting business. Therefore you would need to settle for two separate places – business and private. The same agent who finds you office space, might help with private accommodation or at least recommend you to a colleague who could. The problem of private accommodation is very much a separate issue which will not be dealt with here, merely to remark that you need somewhere within easy commuting distance from the office and the type of local school you choose for your children. It might be more sensible to have the office in Tokyo and live in Yokohama which is only 45 minutes away by train.

Some imaginative foreign businessmen refuse to have an office or live in Tokyo and do both in the Kansai area, in Kobe which is either three hours away by Shinkansen (bullet train) or one and a half by air from Tokyo and much more pleasant to live and work in. It obviously depends upon your type of business. The government is in any case encouraging local companies to move out of the capital. Moreover, no one knows when the next major earthquake, sometime within the next few years, is going to occur! The best advice is, if you do not have to work in Tokyo, don't!

Renting the actual office itself introduces you to local customs: most leases are for two years, you need to pay two years' rent as security, 80 per cent of which you will get back assuming no damage and so on. (For private accommodation key money varies from six to twelve months' rent.) No interest is paid on this key money by the landlord. The estate agent charges a month's rent. Rent is paid at the end of each month for the following month. If you want to renew the lease, the estate agent receives a renewal fee of a month's rent *and* it could be that the key money has to be paid again, in effect 20 per cent of it because you will only get 20 per cent back from the amount paid for the first lease. However before you can sign a lease, you will usually be required to have a Japanese guarantor, that is someone who will guarantee your ability to pay and behave. (This will also be required for extensions to your visa.)

There is little room for negotiation because land prices are usually so high and there is such a demand for office and private accommodation. Get the agent to explain the terms of the lease if in Japanese and study them very carefully if in English, but remember that in Japan, contracts do not have the same validity as in the West. You just have to trust the landlord and hope that he or she will fulfil the terms of the contract. You certainly will be expected to. As you see, right from the start you are committing yourself to large sums of money – unless you arrange only for temporary space from Helpmates or the Jardine Business Centre. Unless you stay in a hotel, you are still going to have to find private accommodation.

However there are clubs, such as International House in Rappongi, where you can stay for half the price of a hotel. But you have to be a member and join like a London club. It might well be worth trying to do this before arrival. It has a very pleasant ambience and is ideal for inviting Japanese guests. It also has a remarkably good library with many business and economics journals and reference works which aid local research. It is very easy to reach from Tokyo main railway station and the centre of town.

Important additional matters like obtaining a local driver's licence can be time consuming. Enquire whether the International Driving Licence issued by your motoring organization is recognized in Japan. If it is, then you can drive in Japan for one year. If not, then you have to spend many hours at the local driving licence office obtaining a Japanese licence. Be prepared to spend a whole day at it, certainly a morning or an afternoon. Comfort yourself on the loss of time with the wonderful slice of local culture which you get for your money. Please remember too that nothing is cheap in Japan, least of all the various permits and permissions which you have to obtain. They all cost multiples of 3000 and 4000 yen and certainly add up.

Opening a bank account can take ages too, if you insist on obtaining a cheque book, which, if it is a Japanese bank, they will not want to give you. The main thing is to open an account, get an account number and a cash card for withdrawing and depositing money from automatic cash dispensers and, when you know how, paying bills electronically. When using the cash dispenser be very careful to use units of 10 000 yen (ichiman yen). It is terribly easy to want to withdraw 100 000 yen and find that you have withdrawn ten times that amount – 1 000 000 (a million) yen! Most cash dispensers are inside and not outside the bank and during working hours there is usually a bank official to help. Instructions will usually be in Japanese, so be careful.

Depending upon the size of your operation, you will need local staff, at least a secretary, someone who can help you with the language. Once you employ local staff, you become part of the system, take on definite local responsibilities. Assuming you make do with a single secretary to begin with, you will need to pay that person a basic wage monthly, plus allowances for commuting, even family and housing allowance. What you also have to pay are bonuses twice a year, approximately two months' salary each time. There is also health, welfare and employment insurance contributions to be paid by the employer. Do take advice on this.

Telephone, fax, telex and office equipment come next. Nippon Telegraph and Telephone Company (NTT) provide the telephone service but you actually have to buy the line which at the time of writing costs 80 000 yen. You can sell it if and when you leave. Long-distance calls are however often cheaper if you have accounts with other companies (KDD for abroad, Nippon Telekom for inland). It may take some time to organize opening accounts with all these companies. Arrange payment of monthly accounts by debit transfer which they will probably require in any case. You can also pay such accounts from an account held at the Post Office. Many people use the Post Office for paying bills because it is cheaper than using a bank.

OFFICIAL PROCEDURE

Depending upon the status of your operation, the notification procedure varies. Basically if you are only opening an office to observe the market, carry out publicity exercises and not conduct any actual business transactions, then no commercial registration or corporate taxation are required. Once you start doing business, then both become necessary. This involves filing notification (as specified in the Foreign Exchange Law) for the following:

1. direct national investment;

2. branch office registration papers;

3. various notifications to the tax office.

Current details of the Foreign Exchange Law should be verified with JETRO or; where possible, the nearest branch of a Japanese bank of which there is an increasing number abroad.

You will need help to understand the forms, even when in English, and in finding the government or municipal offices to which to deliver them. Be prepared to invest a lot of time in the procedures and be pleasantly surprised if it is shorter than you originally feared. My advice is to try and find out all about this before arrival through Helpmates or some other service. You can save so much time by finding out beforehand which other papers or certificates you might require. You only pay corporate tax if you actually conduct business, ie buy and sell. If you do business, after deducting salary, you are taxed on the remaining corporate income on a sliding scale depending on capitalized value of the company and whether or not dividends are paid.

TARIFF ELIMINATION AND TAX INCENTIVE PROGRAMS

The Japanese Government certainly tries to show willing by eliminating tariffs and providing importers with tax incentives.[9] In April 1991 another 1004 items were freed from tariffs and four had tariffs reduced. There was a wide range of items, including those for building, sanitary equipment, fork-lift trucks, lifts and skip hoists, gas and electricity meters, cameras and photographic material, sports equipment (skis) traffic signals for railways or tramways, road-use traffic signals, just to mention a few.

There are also tax credits for manufacturers 'whose value of imports in categories covered by the programme are at least 10 per cent higher than the largest value in a nominated base year',[10] that is 'the financial year within the period of the program with the highest level of total imports to date'.[11] The system is as follows. A manufacturer either chooses a tax credit (5 per cent of the increase in value of imports, yet not more than '10 per cent of the corporate tax for large companies and 15 per cent for small and medium-sized companies'[12]) or an additional depreciation allowance on 'machinery and equipment purchased during or two years prior to the taxable year, and which are still in the company's possession at the end of the taxable year'. There are also tax breaks for wholesalers and retailers 'for the purpose of developing markets for manufactured imports'. The tax credits are calculated on the actual 'increase in the value of imports in eligible (import) categories'.[13] Interestingly enough, even printed books, newspapers, journals and periodicals are included, as are ferrous products.

Notes

1. Johnson, C (1987) *MITI and The Japanese Miracle. The Growth of Industrial Policy, 1925–1975*, Tuttle, Tokyo: 2nd printing.
2. See Friedman, G and Lebard, M (1991) *The Coming War with Japan*, St Martin's Press, New York.

3. JETRO (1989) *A Survey on Successful Cases of Foreign-affiliated Companies in Japan*, p3.
4. ibid.
5. ibid.
6. ibid, p5.
7. ibid.
8. JETRO (1992) *Investment Japan*, Tokyo.
9. See JETRO (1990) 'Items covered by Tariff Elimination and Tax Incentive Programs' *The Business Person's Guide to Japanese Import Promotion*, Tokyo.
10. ibid, p59.
11. ibid, p60.
12. ibid, p59.
13. ibid.

Identifying the Gaps

'Go for the gaps!' is excellent advice, finding them another matter. Where are they? As everyone reading this book now knows, even the most superficial survey of the living conditions of the people and their lifestyle reveals substandard housing, traffic congestion and limited leisure facilities with everything being exceedingly expensive. How can foreign business help? Housing is one gap American suppliers of pre-made houses fill, but such a product is not only dependent upon finding local customers, but local agents, architects and builders and so on. The problem is therefore not merely to produce what people want but also to get some local specialist to arrange things. It is the in-between, go-between part which would be the most difficult. Some gaps are obviously more complicated to fill than others.

Traffic congestion is a problem and yet paradoxically and environmentally perversely enough, the sale of foreign cars, though limited to 2.6 per cent of total market, has increased and has increased potential. Anti-pollution controls are very severe and add expensive complications to importing cars thus the best thing to do is to export cars. It is also forbidden to have a car in Japan unless you have a garage or space to park it. If you want to make an enemy for life in Japan pinch his parking place, a friend lend him or her yours.

Leisure fanatics constitute a gap too – sports goods and clothing – but local competition is severe. Perhaps the obvious gaps are too obvious and thus the most difficult to fill because local manufacturers are more than aware of them.

Undoubtedly the manufacturers of luxury cars, Rolls-Royce, Mercedes and BMW, are learning to fill obvious specialist gaps with distinction or imaginatively. Specialist knowledge is obviously essential, above all flair or simply the sort of design that is different and foreign (eg British china). Perhaps it is not so much bargains the Japanese customers seem to be looking for but for a special kind of excellence.

The problem of introducing your product may initially be making it known. One obviously turns to advertising to find 23 per cent of it in the hands of Dentsu, apparently 'twice as much as that of its closest competitor, Hakuhodo'.[1] Dentsu, which has bought advertising slots from the main television networks then sells them to major clients in automobiles, beer and cosmetics who are competing with each other. The clients don't like it, but what can they do? If they go elsewhere, they will not obtain the sort of coverage they want. The decisions are taken out of their hands and freedom of action circumscribed by the local way of doing things. This is not to say that Dentsu does not do a good job and respect a client's individual needs, but somehow clients must feel that sometimes they would like more of a choice. Or do they? It could be that the Japanese discipline themselves in exercising choice, so that if the service provided by Dentsu is to their liking, they are satisfied. Individuality may not be at a premium. Dentsu, with its near 6000 employees and the largest advertising agency in the world, can be large enough to satisfy competing clients whose real competition with others is to obtain the services of Dentsu.

THE DISTRIBUTION SYSTEM

No matter how good the product you wish to offer on the Japanese market, if you cannot distribute it to the customer, it is a waste of time, effort and expense. However, before railing against the system, it helps to understand the rationale which lies behind it. In one way it is a relic of the days when transport facilities were rudimentary and much industry and commerce, as is still the case, was in the hands of small businesses.

The distribution system is also a web of interlocking relationships, still often family, which characterize an economy suspended between pre- and post-Industrial Revolution. The system may be cumbersome and costly but it can also be very quick providing a 24-hour service to any part of the country[2] and suits the small shopkeepers who have very little storage space and require many small deliveries during the week, some even every day. Moreover the wholesalers share the risk with the retailers by holding stock for them and issuing credit so that the retailer only pays after he has sold the goods in question. In a sense the retailer is only an agent for the wholesaler. The wholesaler therefore has an additional commercial function, more responsibility and costs for which additional markup is made.

The advent of supermarkets, such as Daiei, though resisted by small shopkeepers, has already made inroads into the retail trade and led to rationalization and the amalgamation and thus reduction of the number of wholesalers. With the recent change in legislation, due to American pressure to admit large retail stores from abroad, more rationalization can be expected. If you cannot get your products distributed by the wholesale system, then the supermarkets might be more helpful.

The real problem of distribution is agreeing on returns and payment for goods. As explained above, retailers try to reduce the element of risk as much as possible, especially with foreign products where it is felt that the risk might be even greater. The individual retailer wants the big name wholesaler and distributor who will accept returns and give credit. The Post Office and private carriers will not do that. Solve the twin problems of returns and credit, and the distribution problem itself becomes less formidable.

UNIONS

Unions are not the thorn in the side of industry nor in general are they against introducing labour-saving devices for unpleasant tasks or workers being multi-skilled and operational. They do demand higher wages at the celebrated annual *shunto* time of making wage demands. They protest, their leaders shouting and screaming (literally) at protest meetings. However compared to American or British unions, they are cooperative and conciliatory with management.

Unions were tamed in the great union bust-up with Nissan[3] in 1953 when police and gangsters (*yakuza*) mauled them into submission. The danger then, from the management's and government's side was that Japanese labour would have been brought effectively under the control of communist-dominated unions and, as was argued, local industrial effort would have been reduced and the economy adversely affected.

Whether things would have been as bad as this, no one knows, but undoubtedly the cooperation and conciliatory approach adopted by the unions has helped preserve industrial harmony and thus benefited the economy.

LABOUR: JAPANESE STAFF

The problem with finding good local staff in Japan is no secret. Unfortunately there is no prestige in working for a foreign firm, possibly the reverse. A salaryman will first select a local company because of lifetime employment, assured promotion with age and identification with his own country. With a foreign company, a Japanese employee may feel insecure, never knowing whether or not it will ultimately fold and leave him jobless.

Moreover, the foreign predilection for paying according to results may not suit him at all. It is loyalty to the company and dedication to the job for which he seeks financial reward. The pressures of the job itself are understandable. Uncertainty about his salary and promotion are unusual in the Japanese system and as far as he is concerned unwelcome.

Personnel officers can also cast their recruiting net wider seeking those Japanese who have already studied and/or worked abroad. The trouble with these recruits is that excellent as they may have been abroad, on return home they may well have cultural re-entry problems and be mistrusted by their own colleagues who have never been out of the country.

Casting the net to include those changing jobs can result in taking on misfits. Head hunting mid-career in Japan is a chancy business because the whole local business culture is against it. Good people are usually too identified with their own company which assures them lifetime employment to want to change. The American 'easy come, easy go' approach simply does not suit the Japanese way of doing things. If such an occasion should arise, then obviously it is sensible to employ a reputable employment (head-hunting) consultant to vet such a candidate.

Undoubtedly where a gap in the local employment scene lies is with female candidates who in Japanese companies can often look forward to careers as glorified tea ladies who can be fired at a relatively early age. Of course there are those women who do not want to stay in work long but look forward to marriage and raising a family. Such risks are always involved for the employer. However, Lloyds Bank, whose local manager I spoke to, was enthusiastic on the subject of how successful his policy of employing women in the bank has been. (From my experiences, university employment departments could try more often to introduce the idea of seeking employment with a foreign company to female graduates.)

COMING TO TERMS WITH JAPANESE LAW

The Japanese do not like resorting to law, although today they are increasingly doing so on matters of national importance, such as the religious aspects of the Emperor's recent enthronement. Some people felt that some parts of the ceremony were too reminiscent of times gone by when it was claimed that the Imperial House had divine connections. People felt too that the late Emperor's funeral, paid for by the State, should in part not have been because the State is, according to the Constitution, supposed to be secular and thus allied to no particular religion.

Private people tend to try and avoid disputes and, where they occur, have them resolved by conciliation rather than before a judge in court. Indeed the judge will, if the matter comes to court, urge that this be done.

For the foreign businessperson and employer of local personnel, the labour courts, which may well tend to favour the employee because of the official policy of lifetime employment, could raise difficulties when it comes to dismissing unsatisfactory members of the staff. This is a further reason for proceeding with caution when choosing staff or where a mistake has been made: arranging dismissal in exact accordance with the law and of course doing so in as tactful a way as possible, however exasperating the circumstances.

THE YEN

Business is about many high-flown things, human relations, satisfying customers, but, in the final analysis, it is measured in money, that is currency. There you must get your sums right in yen – which means in dollars too. However if you are doing business on the domestic market, then it is yen which primarily concern you. You have to make a profit in yen, but when balancing the books at head office abroad, then exchange rates are obviously vital. Your concern is with the total effect on overall profitability. Usually the yen appreciates, especially since the Plaza Accord of 1985, but from 1985 to 1991, the yen has depreciated in value. For those doing business inside the country this has an effect, especially on the cost of living.

As a foreigner doing business in Japan, movements in the price of yen could be very important, especially if you are still based abroad or your company is controlled from outside Japan. It is no use investing time, money and effort in basically a declining asset (the currency) unless there are no other compensating factors. In Japan there usually are, but none of the glossy and highly informative brochures published by JETRO or the numerous books I have read really consider the currency aspect of doing business in Japan.

You can as the Americans say 'work your butt off' yet, at the end of the day, have considerably less than expected to show for it. In this connection it would seem to me to be essential to have good bank connections, not only with domestic but also with foreign banks on the spot, so that you can with the latter (there are complications with the former) more easily and quickly move funds abroad if the need arises. When it comes to doing foreign business, local banks are not always very flexible because of the many existing regulations.

ACCOUNTING

Japanese accounting will appear more complicated because a transaction will be recorded three times under:

1.   Advice of delivery note: *Hai tatsu*

2.   Bill: *seikyu-sho*

3. Receipt: *ryoshu-sho*

Even relatively simple transactions like a book refund for purposes of accounting has to have the three above-mentioned documents. The usual form of authenticating a document is the seal (*inkan*) as opposed to the signature. Double-entry book keeping is practised as in the West and there are the equivalent of Chartered Accountants in the local accounting profession. Of course the language used in the accounts is Japanese.

Actual payment or goods may be made in the form of promissory notes (*tegata*) or simply post-dated cheques which are illegal in America but not in England. In Japan cheques seldom bounce. If a cheque is returned to drawer, the bank usually closes the account. If it happens again, presumably at another bank, then there are serious consequences for the drawer which could include facing bankruptcy proceedings. The Japanese bank reacts in panic.

As regards the actual presentation of accounts, the Japanese long-term view of making a profit and the settling of a lower priority on dividends, influences the manner of presenting accounts. According to the Commercial Code, temporary costs, that is variable ones such as for starting up, research and development, are included which enable a company to show its true financial state of health. Moreover Japanese companies, being closely connected to their house banks, are usually chronically undercapitalized in comparison to Western companies.

It is obviously vital to familiarize yourself with local accounting practices, which at the beginning obviously means taking specialist advice though this can be very expensive for the small business.

THE CHANGING JAPANESE MARKET

Getting to know local markets[4] is obviously essential for the prospective foreign importer. As everyone knows the Japanese consumer is price and quality conscious, demanding on the one hand, but appreciative on the other, of good service and willing to pay for it. Young consumers are of great importance today, yet will be less so in the years to come with an increasingly ageing population demanding a different type of product with even more service and convenience. By 1995 it is reckoned that universities will be hard put to find enough students to fill them. Today they are overflowing.

What does this portend for the foreign businessperson? At a guess, it would appear that investment services will be in even greater demand, status exclusive, luxury products even more so and quality will be at a premium, as it is today, but especially so. Brand names in clothing, food and sports equipment for senior citizens will be in greater demand. Golf is one of the sports older people like, one could say among some salarymen, adore, with people actually practising their strokes with their bare hands on station platforms. As there are so many environmental hazards in laying out and maintaining new golf courses in Japan, and membership of clubs, even being able to play a round of golf, is so expensive, many go on golfing holidays abroad. This must be an expanding market, one would have thought, for years to come.

Travelling abroad of course will be stimulated still further. We have to think more in terms of providing greater luxury in our own countries for older Japanese travellers. Our hotels need remodelling. They simply do not match up to new Japanese luxury hotels. We need to concentrate on better service and I feel discourage staff from expecting gratuities. Wages should be increased as compensation. Japanese do not expect to tip. In America and elsewhere tipping is a form of extortion and is demeaning for both the giver and the receiver. We have to return to the old-fashioned idea of service for its own sake, that is if we are to sell our tourist services to the Japanese. We may have to make facilities cleaner, better and smarter. It will pay dividends.

I have to say this: the Japanese are lovely people. Treat them right and they will come back time and time again. They are *not* shifty, they are shy, modest and retiring by nature as individuals. They need to be in a group to feel human and to relax. Somehow we have to adapt to this. A different psychology is involved. Greater study of this by foreign entrepreneurs is required.

With a dynamic market and an increasingly ageing population, greater skill will be required than hithterto, above all a greater knowledge of Japanese culture. The older the people, often the less English they speak. If they do not speak English, then you can forget other Western languages. Great challenges of adaptation lie ahead for the foreign businessperson who wants to increase his share of the Japanese market.

Notes

1. See Leonard Koren (1990) 'Success stories: how eleven of Japan's most interesting businesses came to be', *The Japan Times*, appendix, p165, column 2. Although written in a popular and simple style, this book contains some very useful and interesting basic information on major Japanese companies, as well as foreign entrepreneurs.
2. See article in *The Daily Yomiuri*, 12 August, 1991 ('Labour shortage aids business boom') showing how sales of Distribution Automatic Systems have increased by 20–25 per cent during the last few years.
3. Horsley, W and Buckley, R (1990) *Nippon New Superpower. Japan Since 1945*, BBC Books, London, pp55–7.
4. See the excellent JETRO publication (1990) *The Japanese Market: A*

Compendium of Information for the Prospective Exporter, Tokyo, which should be required reading for any exporter to Japan.

6

Settling Down

James Abegglen, US Professor, Japan hand, business consultant and guru, who is also a very kind man, draws attention to the so-called 'silicon cycle' – 'You go through this enormous growth, then you get a falling off.'[1] While the American reaction may be to reduce commitment or even pull out, Abegglen explains how the Japanese try 'to ride that cycle, invest through it. And as the demand surges, guess who's got the capacity?'[2] Settling down may therefore mean not just consolidating gains but absorbing losses, taking the rough with the smooth but with the added psychological strain of doing it in a foreign environment with very little local support, if any, and head office breathing down your neck or, if entirely locally based, feeling more isolated and desperate than ever.

And the feeling of isolation in what may appear a largely alien community is not to be underestimated. Head-shrinkers for expatriates are in great demand in Japan and head-shrinking itself is no doubt a growth industry. Good Samaritan telephone services are advertised in all the English language newspapers and journals. Alcoholics Anonymous too. Certainly there is no harm in trying them if the need arises. I found, though for different reasons, the municipal Community Service for Foreigners, which exists in some large cities, very helpful when I felt so isolated because of the language barrier. There I found the best teacher I have ever had and it cost nothing. The ones I had had before (four) had been useless and cost my university, which had initially paid for their services, a fortune.

I am not a great believer in expatriate organizations based on expats feeling sorry for themselves and making snide comments about the Japanese. There are Japanese out there who are more than willing to help. They may not be able to put your business on the up and up again, but I do believe that sympathy and understanding give fresh courage, clear the mind and brain, and allow new, creative ideas to enter.

Remember that if you cannot take Japan, the best thing is to get out while you still have your money and your reason. But if you are prepared to compromise then the break will come, given persistence and creative ideas.

STRANGE AND FOREIGN

Perversely perhaps, I have always found the foreignness of Japan – the fact that I can go out into the street and know that no one can understand a word I say nor understand my problems; that the people I hear talking are speaking a language that I can only imperfectly understand – a great help when I am wrestling with a problem by correspondence back home.

I have a great feeling of relief when I am able to ring home so that someone there can put my local problems into some sort of perspective. This is of course personal and not in a strict sense related to business, but in a recent period between posts when I was getting desperate, I found the contact with home of great importance and help. I am sure that in business, too, the same must hold. The point is that the sense of isolation from your foreign surroundings can help solve the problem of your attitude to the problem. Just as it is a great handicap to be a foreigner in Japan, it can also be a great advantage in facing problems which may arise.

It is really a continuation of the mental preparation suggested in the first chapter. In a sense doing business with the Japanese is a constant form of preparation, possibly meditation and reflection too. The Japanese, in preparing their own freshmen for entering business, make use of the Zen-Buddhist temple instruction. It is by all accounts very strict and demanding and I would hesitate to recommend it to Westerners, but the idea of keeping yourself mentally fit now for doing and settling down to do business – that is consolidating achievements as well as dealing with reverses – is very much a case of mental training and psychological attitude. If you undertake this, you are on the same wavelength as the Japanese and better able to do business with them.

THE QUESTION OF COMMITMENT
(DOING BUSINESS IN RURAL AREAS)

Sooner or later when settling down, the question arises of how long for? How long do you intend to stay? It is crucial to success. We will consider this point in discussing relations with head office. Now we wish to consider it in relation to the individual businessperson in Japan. Obviously what was said about having local managers stay for a reasonable length of time applies to senior executives as well, perhaps though, most of all, to small-business owners. Larger companies send people back home, get replacements and substitute local staff. The small-business owner *is* the business. When he leaves Japan, the business goes with him. The Japanese are very aware of this and the question of commitment in length of stay assumes greater importance, though it is important for everyone doing business in Japan. Because it is so significant for the small businessperson, we wish to consider length of stay and thus commitment to the community in connection with the phenomenon of small expatriate businesses in Japan.

SMALL BUSINESSES – CASE STUDY

When I first began to write this book, I imagined that the reader would be from the world of big business, an executive just off to Japan or a manufacturer or senior professional specialist seeking to enter the Japanese market. In a way I felt that the small businessman was not so relevant but, because I have met a number of such people, and indeed as a teacher myself offering my services on the academic market, I was naturally interested in their work and experiences. My membership of the Osaka American Business Association confirmed this and I spent a number of hours plying members with questions about their work and I am afraid exhausting everyone's patience in the process. The president, the inimitable Sandy Taubenkimel, told and taught me a lot, especially when I tried out my theories on him or even presumed to disagree with the results of his distilled wisdom. However, most of the time, I just found myself listening spellbound to the stories Sandy told, enlivened as they were by his native wit, particularly when quoting his mother's advice: 'Dress British and think Yiddish!'

It was he and another member, Chris Christophersen of Amway distributors who made the point that it is the small businessman on his own who really is in the front line in Japan, firing his rifle away with someone else from home handing over ammunition – but that when one looks back for encouragement, one often finds that the helper has gone! One is alone. The small businessman, who may of course have a few assistants, is virtually on his own doing business with the Japanese, often with few resources and without the support of a large company behind him. The small businessman has to succeed to survive and stay in the country. He has to communicate with the Japanese. He has to use all his business skills and they are often in the first instance human.

One example is John Ulmer, an American, founder of Interwood School and Cultural Centre in Minama, a village one and a half hours away from both Kyoto and Osaka by train. The story goes that John first settled in the village, a place of few distractions, to finish off writing his PhD. Having done that, conceived the idea of building a school where 'outdoor English courses' were to be held and while writing Hollywood film treatments with his brother, saved up the money necessary to obtain a loan from a local bank. This impressed the local mayor so much that he was virtually given a plot of land to build the school. He then bought the timber necessary from Canada and America, arranging for its importation and so on, imported labour to construct the building from America, Canada and England and overcame the very considerable opposition to such imports and foreign labour. How he managed all that made fascinating listening and contained many lessons for those embarking on doing business with the Japanese.

Lesson one was that there is considerable business with the Japanese to be done in rural areas. One should not always think of doing business in large cities.

Lesson two was the cross-cultural part: convincing the Japanese that one was there to stay in the community where one lived and operated and show dedication to the community, be this in volunteering to join in communal clearing-up operations on Saturdays, paying for a scholarship for a local child to go to the States, arranging a home stay, attending village meetings and generally joining in.

He admitted that there were some moments where things could have become ugly, such as when he was summoned to a village meeting to explain to incensed villagers and representatives of the local timber and labour associations why he had imported materials and labour. He still remembers vividly the hostile atmosphere which appeared to him to be nearing physical violence. He remembers the steadfastness of the mayor and how the latter's re-election centred on the issue of the school; how the mayor was re-elected unopposed and how that gentleman offered to secure the loan of 50m yen should John ever default on repayments.

John explained how he marketed the idea with the help of the local and subsequently national press, radio and TV which all cost him time, but no money. He also explained how helpful the bank was in recommending potential clients for John's other business endeavours which extended beyond founding an English school. The most interesting thing of all was when he explained that although he was married to a Japanese, he maintained that the greatest mistake of all would have been to use his wife as an interpreter and burden her with all the problems attendant on carrying out the project. He concluded his talk by saying that many people did not succeed in Japan because they really did not approve of the Japanese and that obviously that was the wrong way to seek to do business with them. An air of disdainful patronage would not do. The Japanese do not owe the foreigner a business or even a job. How true.

The senior company executive in his company-rented accommodation complete with Japanese staff at work, can probably get away with being more indirect or less involved with the Japanese. It is not to be recommended, but it can be done. To what extent this can be considered to be 'doing business with the Japanese' is another question. The small businessman does not have such a choice. It is sink or swim. That is why I feel he is so relevant to the subject of this book.

Both Sandy and Chris are married to Japanese ladies. They are established in the country. Sandy made the point, as did John, that you have to show commitment to Japan, no fly-by-night, quick profits, then off back home. You have to be there to stay, but of course, as Sandy again points out, you cannot ultimately give a lifetime's commitment that you want to stay until you die. It may sound far-fetched, but sometimes I get the impression that once the Japanese have accepted you in their midst, literally in John's case, as members of their village (the phrase *mura* is used), then they really expect to bury you as well! The business relationship in Japan is more than business, it is a way of life and without the way of life, you will never really get or do business with the Japanese. Ultimately, you are, in their eyes, no longer a foreigner. You are not a Japanese either, but you have been assimilated and become one of them. This applies to doing business as a foreigner to some extent at least in any country, but one feels especially so in Japan.

What of relations with home, in particular with head office?

RELATIONS WITH HEAD OFFICE

Surely one of the trickiest problems can be relations with head office and theirs with you. If they work, fine; if they do not, sales will plummet or you will have to work ten times as hard to make up for the deficit. There are a number of reasons for this, some of them often forgotten.

Basically head office has to repose full confidence in the man on the spot. How it gives him full authority to act on his own inititiative and at the same time retain control of what goes on in Japan is an art in itself. If head office does not give its local manager full authority, the Japanese customers and clients will soon realize this because of the constant referral of matters to head office for decision rather than making decisions on the spot.

As head office has the ultimate responsibility to shareholders for what goes on, including of course making a profit, and considerable sums are necessarily invested in running the Japan operation, there are many excellent reasons for keeping the reins of control in London, New York or wherever headquarters happens to be. The only trouble is this will not work in Japan.

It is therefore necessary to delegate considerable discretion to the local manager and not only this but to back him up visibly by the visits to Japan by the chairman at regular intervals. It may be expensive in air fares and time-consuming but, from all accounts, it definitely pays dividends. The Japanese like to feel that, particularly with a foreign company with a headquarters many thousands of miles away, they are still being attended to as though they were themselves conducting business in London or New York. Yes, they want it both ways, but they are the customers. If you want their business, that is how it is going to have to be. You have to give them a compelling reason to do business with a foreign company and not with their own people which, of course, they would normally far prefer to do for reasons already detailed above.

The consequences for recruitment policy for staff to work in Japan are obvious. First only send the best staff to Japan, whom of course you would normally far prefer to keep at home. It will be a question of priorities. You have no means of knowing that staff who may be excellent at home will be able to cope with all the cross-cultural problems which may arise in Japan. Great care and expertise in selection is essential but in itself, however good, can never prove an absolute certainty as to a particular person's ability to work in Japan. Gordon Nebeker, an American, who directs the Rothschild's office in Tokyo, told me that you never can tell who is going to prove adaptable in Tokyo, that is who is going to be liked by Japanese clients. There are too many unknown variables. Undoubtedly it takes a special mixture of tolerance, persistence and charm (charisma, if you like) to sell oneself in Japan. And selling the product or service is really selling your own personal relationship to the client, in other words selling yourself.

SELF-EVALUATION

Selecting the local manager is not only a question of evaluating business and personal skills from above but of his evaluating his own, especially his degree of involvement both in the job and the country itself, not only as part of the job but as part of his own private life as well. You either find the Japanese with all their foibles sympathetic, or you do not. If you do not, please get out before irreparable damage to your business and your own self-esteem is done. By all means take your time to decide; do not make hasty decisions as we all tend to do in moments of most frenzied confrontation with Japanese culture. Take your time but be absolutely honest with yourself.

Because you have a 'privileged' position as a foreigner, do not be tempted to imagine yourself as a sort of district officer among colonials or simply assume a colonial stance yourself. It is very easy to do this because you probably do not speak the language and are therefore in a state of communicative isolation. You probably have the inner resources to withstand this, even to enjoy it. Perhaps you have your family with you. You go home, shut the door and might just as well be in Bromley or Long Island. You watch Sky Channel, can view debates in the House of Commons or the news from the States and feel inside still at home many thousands of miles away. Your children go to the local

American or Canadian Academy or international school. What the heck do you need to worry about? You do your job as well as you can. It cannot last forever. Hold on a little longer and you will be transferred back home, hopefully with promotion as a reward for having sweated it out in this 'Mickey-Mouse' country.

Please go now! Do. You are, unbeknown to yourself, doing your company, yourself and possibly members of your family too, incalculable damage. You have to be dedicated in some way to the country itself. You have to feel at one with it. The senior managers and executives I interviewed never said this in so many words, but it was obvious. One was married to a Japanese lady, the other told me how he used to get up every morning at 4 am, to wrestle with the language, and others let me know, with their attitude to things Japanese and their understanding for them, how identified they had become with the country.

This feeling of identification with Japan is not something synthetic, something you can manufacture before arrival however intellectually interested you may genuinely be in Japanese culture. You have to experience it and, so to speak, pass the test. As a test it is one you may fail a number of times. I certainly have. It may take more than conscious effort to succeed. One has to *unlearn* so many attitudes, so many behavioural responses. As these have often become so ingrained with time, the older and more experienced you are, the more difficult it will be. You will probably find yourself going through phases as many books explain: first joy and appreciation at everybody's kindness and welcoming, then realization that you do not quite belong, followed by the so-called '*gaijin* (foreigner's) blues' and then after a period of isolation you either come to terms with it (or assimilate); or give up.

How important is Japan to you? At present it may seem important, perhaps very important, but not of ultimate importance. But what of the future where the global exceeds international business in significance. Doing business in Japan may be its own reward but even if it does not, it offers the precious bonus of learning about how the Japanese do business at home, the better to do business with them elsewhere, be it in competition or in joint ventures with them. Doing business in Japan is therefore of global significance and choosing a local manager thus has or could have global significance.

In the not so very distant future with increased and increasing volume of business moving eastwards, some global companies are going to have to consider moving their headquarters eastward to Tokyo too. I am beginning to doubt whether London or New York, Frankfurt or Paris in the long run are going to be the best centres for trying to run global business (international perhaps) precisely because of the cross-cultural problems involved. This may sound far-fetched but I believe may become inescapable.

Up till now the Japanese from sheer necessity have done us the favour of coming to us. Not all of us have been particularly welcoming. True, Japanese non-tariff barriers have had a dampening effect on reciprocal gestures too, but we have always assumed that the sheer size of the American market and, added to that, the European Common Market dwarfed any posssibility of who ultimately could call the tune. Of course it had to be the West. Population numbers now speak against this with not only the sun rising in the East, but the missions of consumers with money based on growing GNPs as opposed to our own stagnating or scarcely growing economies in the West. The Japanese may be weak on services, which is why they have to buy up the world's banks to make theirs the largest, but we have to admit that in manufactured goods they can often produce better and certainly cheaper. And, as yet, which we are most definitely not, they are prepared literally to pay the price at home with modest living conditions and a high cost of living. And this we in the West, as yet, are not prepared to do. If we cannot beat them, and we do not seem to be able to, we may well have to join them.

All these global considerations, I would argue, are pertinent to choosing the local manager for Japan and thus by extension future chairman of the company. Serving in Japan should, in my view, be a prerequisite for any company chairman, indeed for any manager. What business needs is less management theory and more experience of the countries with impressive management performance – Germany and Japan. I have always felt that the respect accorded to American MBA programmes by Europeans and Japanese, however prestigious the universities which presented them, was misplaced judging by the performance of the American economy.[3] It is the Americans who should study in Germany and Japan; and not vice versa. The practical problem involved is of course language. So few people speak German or Japanese. Surely this has to change too.

Notes

1. Quoted by Killen, P J (1990) in 'Business Talk' about 'Abegglen: Japan Business Adviser' *The Daily Yomiuri*, 9 October, p9.
2. ibid.
3. Kang, T W (1991) *GAISHI: The Foreign Company of Japan*, Tuttle, Tokyo, px.

7

Foreign Companies in Japan

What of the foreign companies in Japan already? JETRO has surveyed five groups and deals with them in five different publications that form a set.[1] (This chapter draws heavily upon the JETRO survey.) These groups are:

1. Industrial machinery and parts, computers and software, electric and electronic appliances, automobiles, ferrous and non-ferrous metals;

2. Foods/food services;

3. Consumer goods;

4. Chemicals and pharmaceuticals, medical supplies, oil products, rubber, glass, textiles, paper products;

5. Commerce, communications, newspapers, publishing services.

The JETRO study shows how in all sectors of the economy (which increased annually since mid-1980 by 4 per cent) imports increased by 65 per cent since 1985, the reasons given being 'the Plaza Accord's effect on exchange rates, the expansion of domestic demand and the development of national policies designed to promote imports'.[2] The figures are impressive with the volume and value of imports doubling; electrical machinery, printing machinery, food-processing machinery, and construction/mining machinery tripling and automobiles increasing 7.4 times. The list reads like a success story which it is. The only reservation is that, seen as a percentage of the economy as a whole, imports remain, with one or two exceptions, very small, especially compared with the volume of Japanese goods exported abroad, particularly to America.

However although the volume may be small when compared with the Japanese economy, seen as a whole with exports, the volume and value of foreign goods are large because of the size of the Japanese market compared to that of importing countries. A small slice of the Japanese market is large in volume for countries such as Britain and Germany. Seen as a cake there is a piece for everyone. Foreign investment has 'more than tripled in value from $930 million to $2,860 million over the same period'[3] but there is no indication that this figure has been adjusted to allow for inflation, yet it does allow for the appreciation of the yen. All the same it is a respectable increase. JETRO puts this down to foreign companies realizing 'the need to make long-term commitments even as the strengthened price competition due to the higher yen provided an immediate incentive.[4]

According to a survey conducted by MITI and quoted in the JETRO survey the foreign profit margin of foreign companies operating in Japan has always been far higher than that of all companies in Japan. But we already know that Japanese companies concentrate on growth rather than profits.

When discussing doing business with Japanese and the challenges and problems involved, it is easy to forget how many major and smaller foreign companies are already doing business in Japan and doing so quite, some of them extremely, profitably. The natural inclination then is to see if lessons can be learned from their experiences, interview the directors and managers, read the glossy handouts and make your own observations. Books on doing business with the Japanese are peppered with quotes and quips from successful foreign businessmen.

What I write I have extracted from literature and on occasion verified with interviews and it is basically second-hand and even if it were first-hand, it might not apply in your case. Yet having said this there is no harm, even much good, in the element of inspiration which can come from reading success stories.

What we are looking for is less a formula which would be too narrow but perhaps more of an approach, an attitude to the problem of doing business with the Japanese which is flexible enough to accommodate individual cases, such as those surveyed by JETRO.

GROUP 1: INDUSTRIAL MACHINERY AND PARTS, COMPUTERS AND SOFTWARE, ELECTRIC AND ELECTRONIC APPLIANCES, AUTOMOBILES, FERROUS AND NON-FERROUS METALS

Advanced Energy One produces power sources for semiconductor manufacturing equipment and was established in the USA in 1981. In Japan it is run by a very independently minded man, Takashi Majima, and he runs it his own way using the resources of the parent company. It is really a joint venture with sales doubling every year. Majima has the financial backing but takes the risk and responsibility. No sales figures were given. The interesting point is the degree of independence enjoyed by Majima and the mutual trust between him and the American parent company. As far as the Americans were concerned, the original problem and solution to it was to find someone of Majima's calibre. The problem of finding local entrepreneurs or staff is a recurring one. To sell or manufacture the product, you have to have the person or people to do it.

Apple Computer Japan, of course a name of world-class renown, competing with every Japanese computer out, but now co-operating on one of its future products with Sony. The interesting thing here is that 'a sizeable percentage of the computers used in Apple computers are actually made in Japan'.[5]

BMW is another world name. BMW's approach was especially significant because the company broke new ground as far as foreign automobile manufacturers were concerned, by establishing its own network of distributors and dealers and so not leaving everything to local importers. The man chosen to do the job was Yoji Hamawaki who had formerly presided over the American subsidiary of Kawasaki Heavy Industries in America, where he developed new concepts for selling motorcycles and, returning home, competed successfully with Honda and Yamaha. He was obviously the man BMW wanted to enter the market in Japan. What held for motorcycles seemed to hold for cars too. Hamawaki set about organizing exclusive dealerships for BMW cars. This was not easy. Hamawaki advertised in the press. Japanese have reservations about advertising in the press for help because it suggests that you cannot help yourself, but he did it all the same and got some unusual offers from companies involved in railways and shipping. Hamawaki wanted successful businessmen, not necessarily automobile experts. However he insisted that whoever became a dealer employed professional staff, provided BMW approved repair facilities and of course the necessary finance. Hamawaki educated dealers in the so-called BMW philosophy. He was demanding. He demanded exclusive handling of BMW cars, no multiple dealerships to which foreign companies importing into Japan often have, at least at first, to submit. He also went his own way on prices and sales – no discounts as is customary in Japan, but correspondingly low loan-interest rates to customers buying cars.

The dealer made his money on increased profit margin rather than on loan interest. Hamawaki also changed BMW's second-hand car market, increasing both the quality of used models to customers and the price to the dealer. Hamawaki showed that it was possible for a foreign company to challenge the system in distribution and sales. He was a Japanese, successfully challenging the Japanese system for a foreign company. One assumes there are not many who could do that. The main thing is that it can be done. All the foreign company has to do is find the right man. So often finding good local staff is a great problem.

Its solution must be in a number of cases a key to success: get the wrong man and the company can lose a fortune before you start doing or rather missing and losing business.

Braun, another German company now a household name in Japan for razors, had the problem of finding an opening into the sales channel. It was particularly difficult at first because, as marketing director, Takashi Fujiwara, explained 'a lot of electrical shops and wholesalers literally belonged to one of the big manufacturers, so that they wouldn't really deal with products from other makers.'[6] The answer was to find unaffiliated wholesalers, electrical shops and department stores. One imagines it was the department stores which gave Fujiwara his first real breakthrough because they would be by definition large enough to be independent. Fujiwara also introduced the idea to retailers of special-offer presents, such as Braun's own original bag, to give away with shaver sets. Extensive advertising helped implant the image of the Braun 'close shave' in people's minds. Japanese men do not in fact have such strong beards as Westerners, but this does not prevent Braun claiming a 40 per cent share of the local market with its 'quality' shave. The Japanese appreciate quality and are prepared to pay for it, Braun razors usually being more expensive than most local makes.

Carl Zeiss Co, yet another German company, who as a celebrated manufacturer of lenses and cameras in Europe has to contend with considerable competition from Japanese camera manufacturers, has successfully entered the lion's den but in such a way as to avoid direct competition with Japanese manufacturers in the Japanese market by only offering 'highly advanced products for specialist and industrial use'.[7] In other words they sell the best with an 80 per cent Japanese staff. The key here to success is quality.

Electrolux, the vacuum cleaner, sewing machines and system kitchens manufacturer, sells direct to houseowners, door to door, but also has a mainstream sales channel via Sharp Corporation. Electrolux recently only sold 15 billion yen (1 per cent of its global sales) in Japan but aims to increase this to 10 per cent.

An English company, Spirax Sarco, which manufactures steam valves and has 30 per cent of the world market, not being used to the Japanese distribution system, and having three English general managers, did not produce exciting sales to begin with. Like Advanced Energy Japan, it was decided to pick a good local man who knew the valve business – Mitsuyoshi Shizukuishi. He cracked the local distribution problem and even had the brochures translated into Japanese! He also solved the employee angst of working for a foreign company, that is worrying about being fired. He gave job security to those who worked and earned it. Now the 80 year old English company is in business in Japan.

One important ingredient in the way the Hilti Corporation, a

Liechtenstein company, became established some 50 years before, is what local president Egbert Appel calls 'Mehrwert' (increasing value), using the German expression, that is making the product, in his case 'solving fastening problems in building construction, shipbuilding, industry, interior finishing and civil engineering',[8] usable by teaching customers how to use the equipment – for example anchor systems, drilling and electric tools, diamond drilling tools and construction chemicals – available to customers. In other words, not just selling Japanese customers a product but showing them how to use it with confidence and skill. The Japanese appreciate service, especially when it is provided by a foreign company, which, because it is based many thousands of miles away, might otherwise be considered to be less able to provide the same sort of comprehensive service provided by local competition.

Finding the gap was the secret of Höganäs, a Swedish manufacturer of iron powder produced from iron ore and atomized powders from molten metal. It is used by most Japanese car manufacturers to make heads in VTRs and for pantographs for electric trains. What is particularly interesting is that, when they began operations in Japan, they had 100 per cent of the market but now only 20 per cent as the Japanese began to make cheaper iron powder from scrap iron. Höganäs answered its early problems by building its own plant locally and automating it, thus reducing costs while becoming more integrated into the Japanese economy and community. Sales grew by 14 per cent annually.

Kaercher Cleaning Systems Co Ltd, headquartered as Alfred Kaeracher GmbH & Co, in Munich Germany, had a similar experience to Hilti in profiting from educating local customers about the product, in this case high-pressure hot or cold water cleaning based on using the right type of detergent. The other excellent sales ploy is that Kaercher's cleaning equipment is apparently smaller, more compact and thus handier to use than that produced locally. At the beginning sales difficulties were encountered, but demonstrations convinced potential customers. Again detergents are the key to success, Kaercher itself being in the oil business back in Germany. Local competing manufacturers of such cleaning equipment are apparently not so versed in the use of detergent. Kaercher supplies cleaning units for the JR Shinkansen, Mercedes Benz (cleaning off thick, old wax on imported models and rewaxing) and, it is hoped, soon the Japanese Self-Defence Forces to clean tanks. The Japanese are such clean people and everything that can be kept clean is, perhaps the basic reason why Kaercher is so successful. Strangely enough, the only serious competition Kaercher has is from a Danish manufacturer who mercifully only sells through a local agent.

Micro Focus Ltd, a relatively new company, first established in the

UK in 1976, specializes in marketing COBOL, the standard language for programming business computers. It set up Micro Focus Japan Limited in 1984 and sells to NEC, IBM Japan, Fujitsu, Unisys Japan, Toshiba, Matsushita Electric Industrial, Mitsubishi Electric Corp, Hitachi, Casio, Ricoh and Canon. Who else is there? The interesting thing is that, as Hiroshi Tajima, the deputy general manager of Micro Focus Japan, explained, Micro Focus 'didn't do anything really special for Japan'.[9] However of course Micro Focus obviously did when it set up locally. Yet, Tajima is certainly right when he emphasizes that above all it is the excellence of the products which counts. Yet there must be a number of cases where an excellent foreign product is not sold because it is not offered locally in a fully committed way.

NCR (National Cash Register) has been involved in Japan since 1935 on contract with Nippon Kinsen Torokuki, then later established its own local subsidiary National Kinsen Torukiki but merged during the war (for obvious reasons) with Nippon Kinsen Torokuki to form Nippon National Kinsen Torokuki. In 1951 NCR injected foreign capital into the company by taking up a large part of a capital issue, the first introduction of foreign capital into Japan after the war, and with the subsequent change of the company's name to NCR Japan Ltd, owned 70 per cent of the capital of the company. That is especially significant because it is usually virtually impossible for foreigners to take over local companies. Of course 1951 was a watershed year being the first time after the war that foreign companies were allowed unrestrictedly to remit profits home.

NCR claims a 70–80 per cent share of the POS (point-of-sale) systems used in local department stores, but involvement in the distribution industry is only 30 per cent of total sales, the highest ratio being banking and finance – 50 per cent – where NCR combined customer deposits and withdrawals (hitherto separate in the combined 'teller system'). Basically their main work in this field has been simplifying existing operations, for example 'recirculating' bank notes in automatic teller machines so that money deposited by one customer could be withdrawn by another without the bank having to collect deposited notes and resupply the withdrawn ones in two separate operations.

One of NCR's main tasks is to interface between different types of computers, though MITI is now going to make this mandatory, much to the benefit of the customer.

All this shows how vital for Japanese commerce and industry foreign companies and their products are. It is usually claimed that the Japanese will only joint venture until they have mastered the foreign technology and then discontinue full cooperation. Of course NCR owning 70 per cent of the capital means that the company in Japan, though run more-or-less exclusively by Japanese staff, is a foreign-owned company.

However one imagines that it is the long history of NCR's involvement in Japanese business that has enabled it to assume such a powerful position in the country.

Nihon Valid Logic Systems is a very significant venture because it features an American system of computer-aided engineering (basically setting up computer packages, originally software, and now, in Japan, including hardware) managed, marketed and organized in Japan by a Japanese, Koichi Terasawa, who like Takashi Majima (see p 90), insists on running things his, that is the local way. It seems to be the ultimate solution to integrating foreign with local business ventures. But more significantly too, Terasawa combines American and Japanese management techniques. He personally recruits *and* fires staff to ensure that (a) he only chooses those he does not have to fire and (b) he can demand a failure is not permitted' attitude. Unlike most Japanese companies, he pays special, not just the normal bonuses, on results. Originally it was thought that the company would take three years to make a profit, but it made one right from the start. It seems the ideal marriage between American and Japanese business culture. The question is, how much can this be emulated?

Trumpf, a European manufacturer of quality sheet-metal processing machines, set up a subsidiary when the market in Japan had reached its nadir. The owner Berthold Leibinger understood that Japan was converting from the production of mass to high-quality products, which was what he had to offer local manufacturers himself. As local president Haruo Yosioka says: 'We help customers understand that they will surpass their rivals if they use Trumpf machines. We also do everything we can in regard to after-sales service, in order not to lose out to Japanese companies.'[10] Yosioka is not into merely selling customers a product for its own sake, but as an adjunct to helping a customer improve his own quality of production and increase sales. To put this policy into practical effect, Trumpf has a joint venture with Ishikawajima-Harima Heavy Industries (IHI) called IHI Trumpf Technology, which began producing at Yokohama in 1990. Moreover Trumpf does not just sell a product imported from abroad but develops a number on the spot. Thus over half Trumpf's products have been created within the last few years, proving his flexibility.

GROUP 2: FOOD, FOOD SERVICES

If ever there was a test of a foreign company's ability to enter local markets, then surely food is one of them. Japanese cuisine is so distinctive including as it does raw and even live fish. Moreover seaweed is a delicacy. If you can enter this market, then surely you have attained the necessary cultural business sensitivity to compete in Japan.

The brief case studies given below show how a combination of persistence, patience and at times sheer size can count. Above all though, it is essential to come to terms with local market conditions even though this may involve breaking with tradition and encountering local resistance. The best way to do this is to enter into a joint venture with a local company.

An English teacher Stephen Cooke started up a British restaurant called '1066' in Tokyo with his wife, Jane, who had formerly worked in the hotel and catering trade. Although they have seasonal quiet periods the business flourishes. This is surely an achievement because there cannot be all that many homesick expatriates yearning for English cuisine. They must make inroads into the local population. They are selling English culture too.

The Cookes are unlikely to expand and make millions. They do not have an idea which will sell a millionfold, but they represent single entrepreneurship and show that it can survive in Japan. They had the usual difficulties trying to get 'space'. 'We kept going to a real estate agency everyday for a few weeks until they understood that we were serious. The same is true with banks. You just keep pushing until they take you seriously, and once the barrier is broken, everything becomes normal.'11 Persistence counts, a quality the Japanese respect within reason.

From the smallest to the largest. General Foods of America the world's largest foodstuff maker was established locally as a 100 per cent owned subsidiary in 1954, then in 1973 merged with Ajinomoto Co Inc and is now doing busines as Ajinomoto General Foods Inc (AGF). Merging is blending into the local landscape, being less foreign in the process, 'piggy-backing'12 on the Ajinomoto name and by using Ajinomoto's sales channels as well as the local consensus decision making. Staff are 100 per cent local. Again the ideal way: the foreign company provides the goods, the ideas, the capital and lets the Japanese run it their way. From the Western point of view it is the right way as long as a profit is made fairly quickly, though this is not the Japanese way. However as in Nihon Valid Logic Systems, so it is claimed with General Foods, certain American and management techniques are used such as market studies (although the Japanese have them too). Above all there is an insistence on quality and great attention paid to detail in regard to labelling, packaging and so on.

Cargill North Asia is an interesting example of a company which specializes in what by all accounts the Japanese are determined to keep out: agricultural products; and yet according to local president Evan B Williams, his company is making a success of it. His great hope is in being able to import more beef now that import restrictions have been lifted. He also imports fruit juice. As Cargill North Asia acts like a *sogo-shosha*, because it deals in so many different products (natural rubber, non-ferrous products, wheat, soyabeans, feed grains, oilseeds, sugar, honey and salt), it can afford to wait for beef and citrus markets to grow.

Cargill is also a noteworthy example of a company which experiments to meet local requirements in 'developing new seed varieties'.[13]

Coca-Cola is a name known all over the world and has become firmly entrenched in Japan. In 1914 it used to be an 'expensive imported delicacy' and from 1946 was only supplied to the Allied Occupation Forces until 1959, when it was sold by Nippon Inryo Kogyo which the following year became Coca-Cola Japan and in 1960 began to produce the Coca-Cola concentrate locally.

The setting up of countrywide bottling plants followed until 1963 when local production with sales and marketing became comprehensive. In 1988 Coca-Cola ranked 99th among Japanese companies and number one among foreign-affiliated firms. It owns 92 per cent of the cola drink market (Fanta 85 per cent of the fruit-flavoured sodas). In 1972 Coca-Cola became the first foreign-affiliated company to join the Federation of Economic Organizations and 1973 joined the Federation of Employers' Association.

Coca-Cola's success has been due to its having managed its own automatic machine market and thus assured itself of the most effective form of distribution to the single self-service customer, literally the man on the street. In the country there is a profusion of automatic vending machines some of which even sell hamburgers! (Incongruously enough there is one outside the New Otani Hotel, Osaka. Indeed it is one of the delights of Japan to be able to go out of an expensive hotel and have a snack of noodles on the street outside. Some hotels actually have snack dispensing machines inside. Almost all hotel rooms have tea making facilities.)

Coca-Cola's setting up of a bottling network was vital too and this in collaboration with the shareholders of the bottlers: large conglomerates such as Mitsui and Mitsubishi, the megabrewery Kirin, the Dai Nippon Printing Co, Nichirei Corp, Showa Denko KK, Jujo Paper and Ricoh Co.

The bottlers were responsible for setting up their own sales bases which challenged the traditional wholesale system and the challenge reportedly met with resistance but was obviously overcome. Size helped. Undoubtedly, the larger the company and the more financial resources it has, the more able it is to either overcome local resistance or a favourite phrase, to 'enhance' the work of others in the same field, that is come to some arrangement with them.

Denny's is yet another household name and as such was licensed by Ito-Yokado opening in Japan in Yokohama in 1988. There are 320 stores' of which eight are franchises. Although the Japanese took considerable trouble to learn the American way of operating Denny's, they operate it independently from Denny's USA, though they keep each other informed.

The Japanese provide the local *o-shibori* (hot moist towels which are so refreshing when one enters a restaurant from the heat) and American free coffee refills (not a local custom) and add Japanese culinary effect to the otherwise American style cuisine.

Outside local food manufacturers provide the food according to Denny's recipes but, apart from rice, fresh vegetables and fruit most of the food comes from abroad: frozen green beans from Hong Kong, shrimps from Thailand, and frozen French fried potatoes and pre-cut frozen steaks from America. Denny's whole concept is thus dependent upon being able to import food. Its sale is however restricted by the local tendency not to eat out as much as in America (13–15 per cent of total money spent on food on dining out as opposed to 40 per cent in the USA).

Kentucky Fried Chicken caters for takeaways (which amount to 78 per cent of sales) and young customers who want to eat quickly and cheaply. It is definitely fast food. Its growth after the initial popular exposure at the Osaka Expo '70 was followed by the opening of its first store in November 1970. It now has 850 outlets. However, the problem was positioning the restaurants in busy (and not suburban) areas. Then expansion was rapid. Yet only a third of the outlets is directly managed the majority being franchised. Before becoming franchised Kentucky Fried Chicken does a market-and-feasibility study and then if satisfied insists on three to six months training of the manager of the outlet. Adequate 'capital, store and personnel training have to be assured before the franchise is finally awarded.

Ownership is 50 per cent Kentucky Fried Chicken and 50 per cent Mitsubishi. As Ichiro Takatsuki, a local company spokesman said: 'just because we are a food service company doesn't mean that the Japanese investor has to be from the same industry. On the contrary, there are examples of unsuccessful partnerships which were formed with food service industry companies. The thing which will become the most solid foundation is a relationship of trust with your partner'.[14]

What is so interesting about Kentucky Fried Chicken is that so much of the American image has been retained in the colonial style restaurants, even down to the pictures on the walls and Colonel Sanders standing guard outside. In this way it has a much more distinctive foreign, that is American, image than say Denny's. This appears to be advantageous. It would be interesting to know what effect it has on the young devotees who sit there munching their fried chicken, while they do their homework.

A number of young schoolgirls work behind the counter and then spend their wages, at least partly, eating there after their shift finishes. Part of Kentucky's appeal must be to young people simply giving them employment and somewhere clean and reasonable to sit around afterwards. Kentucky's only problem as far as the chicken is concerned is that it is a little too greasy. Kentucky also has a home-delivery service as do many pizza outlets.

McDonald's has become a byword in Japan for fast food too. McDonald's Corporation has more than 11,000 sales outlets in 53 countries. In 1989 there were 706 in Japan, where it was established in 1977 as a joint venture with Fujita Shoten. The first branch was on the first floor of the Ginza Mitsukoshi store. Though the Japanese Big Mac tastes much the same as the American, there have been some adaptations made to local taste.

Nestlé, another household name, had the problem of sales of hot instant coffee shrinking during the summer months and so introduced instant iced coffee and offered refrigeration bottles for keeping iced coffee cool at the beach or on a picnic. This did the trick. Sales leapt. Then came the so-called 'coffee wars' with competitors introducing condensed coffee which apparently was quicker to make than Nestlé's powdered instant. Nestlé also entered the local breakfast cereal market and included those with vegetable content (Yasai Time), which amounts to half the market share of their cereal products. Local chairman Hyntz J Sinniger, adopted Japanese management structure and has come to terms with the local distribution system saying that 'once you are part of the Japanese system, it becomes your strength'.[15]

Nestlé took over the English confectionery manufacturers Rowntree Mackintosh in 1988 which in 1973 had signed a technology support agreement with Fujiya, local confectioners who operated a restaurant chain, to produce KitKat locally. The original agreement with Rowntree Mackintosh was then developed into a joint venture between Nestlé and Fujiya, with the former holding two-thirds and the latter a third share. While the new joint venture will continue to produce certain products locally, others will come straight from the UK and be marketed independently and not through Fujiya. What encourages Nestlé Mackintosh is that import duty on foreign chocolates was lowered from 20 to 10 per cent in 1989. The problem with chocolates imported from abroad many thousands of miles away and often a long sea voyage is that the quality can deteriorate.

This group's ethos can be summarized by a quote from Shoji Matsuura, associate manager of Ajinomoto General foods: 'if you are going to do business in Japan, I would like you to learn at least the Japanese way of doing things first. Problems will not be solved just by debating difference in cultures and systems.[16] However this does not mean that a foreigner cannot innovate within the system, whether he criticizes it or no. Bernard Leibovich, who presides over Arcane Limited, a French/Japanese company which imports exclusive gourmet products, emphasizes: 'Here in Japan, the longer you are in the market, the more credibility you can get',[17] and at the same time 'from a specialist's point of view, the Japanese food industry still lacks technology and know-how in producing high-quality products in large quantity.[18] In other words, he found a gap.

GROUP 3: CONSUMER GOODS

Faber-Castell, the German pencil manufacturer, made 1.25 billion pencils in 1989, which was more than the total number of pencils produced in Japan (1.19 billion) where the market is very competitive because the Japanese produce their own writing instruments and the market is shrinking. Uichi Tamura, vice president of Faber-Castell in Japan, concentrates on projecting an image of a professionally used and high-quality product. Cosmetic pencils are also sold for use by local cosmetic companies as own brands. Tamura came to Faber-Castell some eight years ago, went to great personal trouble (even answering a questionnaire returned by customers in long hand), increasing sales outlets and targeting business executives for the Alphamatic mechanical pencil. Now sales of that pencil exceed home sales in Germany. Again, Faber-Castell got the right man to do the job.

Exclusiveness in design and quality in foreign products plus exclusive sales ambience, such as in expensive hotel shopping arcades, sell products, such as French Baccarat crystalware. No discounting is allowed, no participation in department store bargain stores. Sales figures are not quoted but one imagines quality sells itself, but whether at an overall profit is not disclosed.

Cultural differences have been mentioned a number of times already. Leisure in Japan is the great growth industry of the future. This is a niche for a British company like B B Martine to fill with high-performance motor boats. The owners Peter Billingham and Ivan Brackin even sold the boat used in the James Bond film, *Living Daylights*, to a Japanese housing company.

Undoubtedly the Japanese are quality conscious. You cannot sell them inferior goods or if you do, only once. However when it comes to taste, that is Western taste, the Japanese are less discerning and will sometimes buy what can only politely be called 'kitsch'. There is a large market for it. The prospective Japanese venture company, Mitsui & Co, was unsure, even pessimistic about sales of particular china figurines; however ultimately it agreed to try and sell them on the domestic market. Yet this was done only after a very expensive advertising campaign in women's magazines by the president of the company, Toshiaki Ishikawa, who had had such difficulty in persuading Mitsui to become involved. His difficulties continued: Mitsui agreed to distribute the merchandise but apparently would not help carry or even display the goods for sale in stores, which is the normal custom in Japan. Ultimately Mitsukoshi, a leading department chain store, later others, Takashimaya and Matsuzakaya, accepted the figurines and they became a success story so that Mitsui became more willingly and comprehensively involved. The moral of the story is that again the right Japanese man on the spot, persistence in negotiation and advertising creating the right image, with of course the appropriate product, will win through in the end however sceptical the local distributor may be. Even the great names worldwide do not always have a clear run to begin with if the local distributor and venture partner is not convinced about local demand for the product.

A great name, associated with luxury, could with Japan's virtually classless society, only appeal to a very select group of customers and thus on balance not provide a sufficiently profitable market. If one then attempts to broaden the customer base to increase sales, the 'prestigious image' could suffer. Cartier, for example, admits that they only sell 10 per cent of overall business on the Japanese market, but of course, this leaves much room for growth the more prestige-conscious Japanese customers become. The problem would appear to be local competition too. Local products are very skilfully made to look prestigious even though they do not always have the name to go with them. Moreover it could be that the Japanese are familiar with some great names but not necessarily all. Or if they are, there are others to be had more cheaply. Other luxury goods firms have also had their problems.

Givenchy sells its luxury travel goods by licensing agreements with local retail and fashion companies. Givenchy experienced the ridiculously high costs of maintaining business, and difficulty in hiring good Japanese staff, though admitting that distribution problems were not much easier in France. The fact that society is classless and average income is high works in Givenchy's favour: 'You can criticize the Japanese system for creating a barrier to doing business here, but you cannot criticize Japanese consumers for imposing high standards on product quality and performance,' says the local president, Patrick Cherrier.[19]

Louis Vuitton's products used to be sold by local distributors in Japan under a sales policy of selling a smaller volume at a higher price, which led to customers, who by definition also shopped in Paris on visits abroad, being able to buy the same product more cheaply there than back in Japan. Traders then bought in Paris too and resold in Japan in the form of parallel import which caused confusion and damaged the image. Vuitton therefore established its own company in Japan and reduced the price gap between Paris and Japan, but with no discounting. One of their greatest problems is however dealing with counterfeiting of their products which does not only occur in Japan (however in Higashi Osaka, a major factory was producing tens of thousands of Louis Vuitton counterfeits per month). From personal observation of Japanese shop staff and junior office staff, there must be other factories in business producing bags and cases which have the 'Vuitton look'. How you define counterfeiting is probably easy in law but in fact not so. You do not need a Vuitton label on a bag to suggest to others that it has the 'Vuitton look', even if it is not the original. Indeed after a time the casual observer might not be able to recognize the original without the label. It is surely this virtual destruction of the image of exclusiveness which is the real damage wrought by tricksters.

Kiwi boot polish is known the world over. Kiwi Japan was only established in 1986 although Kiwi products had been on the Japanese market since before the war. The interesting difference in selling such a fundamental as boot polish on the Japanese market to customers, whose shoes rival any British sergeant major's in shine, is that they require a hard, shiny, wax rather than a traditional soft, spreadable polish. And, of course, the product has to be 100 per cent perfect. Apparently distribution efficiency is being tackled as the existing wholesale network is not as advantageous as the usual one for Japanese manufacturers of shoe care products, who have direct-to-retailer distribution channels.

What is a distribution problem for some foreign companies is not a problem for others. LEGO, a Danish toy manufacturer is, in the words of its manager, more than satisfied: 'I do not think of the Japanese distribution system as complicated and difficult to use ... there is probably no other country in the world which has a system so efficient that products can be distributed throughout the entire country in a single week's time.[20]

Levi Strauss is not dissatisfied either – in the long run. There were initial sales difficulties. However one significant point is that the company insists that bills are paid within 20 days and not 90 as is usual in the local apparel industry. Levis is also apparently unique in using regional wholesalers but as a late-comer, they had to. In so doing they became deeply involved in the system. It now pays dividends.

Melitta, the coffee machine makers, are selling in a market where the taste for coffee is still growing. The traditional non-alcoholic drink, which accompanies most business negotiations, is Japanese green tea, bland but restorative. Melitta had a problem when they found that Japanese people sometimes put the (glass) pot directly on an open fire.

Price is obviously of supreme importance where competitors produce similar goods of similar quality; and new and more efficient manufacturing processes are reducing costs and prices too, especially in a seasonal market such as skis and ski equipment and clothing. If you virtually only have a few months to sell stock before the next season brings new designs, retailers are under great pressure to juggle with prices, sometimes with reductions from 30–60 per cent. 'List prices have come to mean almost nothing.' Customers get confused, especially when, as Luciano Cohen, president of Nordica Japan, subsidiary of the Italian parent company, confirms, supply is far greater than demand, even though his firm's sales have increased by 64 per cent since 1985. The question is has profit increased proportionately?

Japanese skiers constitute, as yet, only a very narrow segment of the population. However the important factor in selling skis in Japan is the increasing preference among young people to hire rather than own skis because of the shortage of space at home, the trouble of transporting them and of course avoiding the necessary capital investment in a product which changes every year.

GROUP 4: CHEMICALS AND PHARMACEUTICALS, MEDICAL SUPPLIES, OIL PRODUCTS, RUBBER, GLASS, TEXTILES, PAPER PRODUCTS

Amway, which sells a variety of detergents, cosmetics, cooking ware and nutrition productions, does so through its own network of distributors who sell them to their friends and receive 30 per cent off the regular price for their pains. At first Amway did this through expatriates living in the country with working visas. Amway then penetrated Japanese society and so a much larger portion of the market. Sales have achieved growth rates of 86 per cent in 1987 and 22 per cent in 1988 with a flattening out in 1989. New products and business tie-ups are now being sought and considered. This type of selling through a network of friends and thus bypassing normal distribution and retail networks obviously has its advantages, but perhaps disadvantages too – because it is limited to a certain type of business person who to a great extent has to combine salesperson and customer in one. Doing business with friends requires a certain kind of product and friend. It does not appeal to everybody if only because so many people do not have the time. Competition for the products must also be extreme in the market and it must be very difficult always to be able to compete in price and quality to remain distinctive. However there is a convenience for one type of customer and a sort of camaraderie which some find appealing, others possibly rather cloying. It will be interesting to see whether this method of selling appeals to the pronounced Japanese feeling of team spirit at work and in the community. However, at home, the Japanese remain very private people. Avon cosmetics are sold door to door but the 'Avon ladies' have learnt that packaging, even the lettering on the label, can affect sales. Various changes also had to be made to products to adapt them to local climate and skin texture. Sales, as reported, boom with turnover for 1989 running at 38.6 billion yen and profits 5 billion yen.

Castrol, the British oil (lubricants) company aims for quality-conscious customers, as they do elsewhere, but with the aid of considerable advertising to educate the public. (Castrol spends 15 per cent of sales revenue on advertising.) The local distribution system was a problem so Castrol set up its own and thus was able to expand with sales going directly to retail outlets. The advice the local president of Castrol, Masahiro Hashimoto, can offer foreign companies is: 'You can't just march in here with the vague notion that you want to sell something in Japan. Get out there and find out what people want!'[21] and he could have added, if they don't want it, educate them by advertising – if you can. Again an example of the right man on the job who knows how to tackle the problem on the spot, is not defeatist, but positive in his attitude.

GROUP 5: COMMERCE, COMMUNICATIONS, NEWSPAPERS, PUBLISHING, SERVICES

Providing services for the Japanese

Providing services to the Japanese is both an art and a skill on its own because you are not selling an inanimate product but something intangible, and personal, even intimate. Whatever it is, whether it is investment advice, where a local customer could best invest his or her money abroad, teaching a Japanese person English, providing a vacation abroad, even just a rapid form of communication, there is bound to be an element of trust on the part of the Japanese customer or client in the foreigner offering and, one hopes, ultimately providing the service. And the Japanese do not automatically trust or necessarily warm to a foreigner as they do to their own countrymen. So much is obvious but perhaps more pronounced with them. Although of course in matters of investment, the average Japanese probably has a healthy scepticism towards some local investment houses.

The winning of trust is therefore essential and the only way to do this is to provide good service but again, because you are dealing with intangibles it is not always possible to satisfy in such a way as one would always wish. The Japanese are not complainers by nature so it may be that the only sign you have of dissatisfaction is that you lose the customer.

British Cable and Wireless needs little introduction and has 120 years' experience behind it, yet it was really only allowed into the Japanese market when the local Telecommunications Act was passed in 1985. The communications market is a particularly large and lucrative one and is now subjected to foreign challenge which has reduced the cost of overseas calls considerably and is continuing to do so every day (hitherto that market was virtually monopolized by KDD (Kokusai Densin Denwa)). With a formerly government-controlled, now privatized national telephone service, with a number of competing ones, there is also a lucrative trade in providing equipment – which foreign countries have also been restricted in entering.

The Berlitz Schools of Languages (Japan) is distinctive and known the world over as a means of teaching foreign languages. Seventy-five per cent of its students take private lessons and so Berlitz competes less, according to local president, Jacques Meon, with local language schools which tend to concentrate more on group or class teaching. It would be interesting to see statistics on this. The other question is which language is being referred to: Japanese or English? There seem to be many grey areas in the teaching of both languages in Japan. English is taught by foreigners from many different countries because no doubt, in the minds of many Japanese, any foreigner can by definition speak English, the world language. Certainly many an American or English lady or gentleman will try their hand at teaching just to earn a living confident that though their pedagogical skills may be few, at least they can speak the language which a number of local teachers of English find it very difficult to do.

Considering Berlitz raises the question of what to charge for language lessons. Berlitz tends to be at the higher end of the scale though not as expensive as some local expatriate competitors. Teaching languages is in any case so nebulous. You are offering a service for which the customer pays but never really knows whether he or she has benefited, until a great deal of money has been spent, and then can never be certain that had the money been spent elsewhere it would not have been better invested. The most important point of all is that the teacher or the school can only do so much. The student has to do 90 per cent or more of the work. Again with languages, it is not the work you do at home which counts, but the opportunity and determination to *practise* the language which are so important.

A language school is therefore selling at best a very incomplete service however much is charged, unless it is residential or somehow geared to ensuring that the student is fully immersed in the language for a length of time. Berlitz attempts this with some of its courses and the Scott's School of Languages does the same. Neither course is cheap and the trouble with this method is that though the learning curve is very high during the course, a student's ability tends to wane if the language is not maintained afterwards. From the pedagogical point of view, the language school business is a very difficult one; from the financial, there is considerable competition.

Local schools charge hefty registration fees on top of course fees (of questionable morality because if a student is not satisfied with a course, he or she loses both). Schools themselves complain that students simply do not turn up to classes regularly, very seldom or sometimes not at all. Running a school involves long-term investment and so on, but undoubtedly there are a number of black sheep in the business, which is a pity for those who genuinely want to learn a foreign language or teach the language.

The basic problem in Japan is that foreign languages are taught too theoretically at school. This particularly applies to the teaching of English which is just an examination, that is a grammar and translation subject, with little or no spoken content. After 10 years at school pupils still can speak very little, if any, English and they can certainly understand virtually none. Foreign languages are not taught to be spoken. Thus the vital element of communication is missing. Indeed what one learns in school is *not* to speak English.[22] This in turn influences the standard of Japanese teaching to foreigners which is very inadequate because there again the element of communication is so often missing.

We have gone into this in some detail as background information to what Berlitz and other language institutes are trying to do: tie the teaching of language to business needs, 'aiming toward the creation of a comprehensive language service business'.[23] As mentioned elsewhere language itself is a great non-tariff barrier.

For those interested in opening a language school as a business, there are a number of factors to be taken into consideration, mainly the intense competition in the larger cities and towns which is mainly where the customers are. Officially there are also a number of administrative hurdles to jump over and the Government is becoming more strict as the reputation of some people in the business becomes more tarnished.

Research suggests that the best way is only to open a school in an urban area where you have something distinctive to offer, otherwise open a special type of school and education centre or open a school in a suburb *with* a Japanese to look after admin and PR. Of course you can start off anywhere with private pupils and work up from that. But this is not really an established business or school as such. Teaching can be a useful adjunct to running another type of business, like the expatriate who runs a second-hand furniture business mainly buying from expatriate leavers and selling to expatriate arrivals. But every Thursday he shuts the shop promptly and goes off to teach.

The tourist business

Everyone knows Club Méditerranée, but to begin with, any seller of vacations to the Japanese has to resolve certain cultural problems, as Yoko Meguri, a communications manager for Club Méditerranée, explained: 'The problem lies in the difference of travel habits between those of Japanese and Westerners due to cultural differences between East and West. Vacations meant sightseeing to the Japanese, and they did not readily grasp the concept of "vacation" as it is understood in the West.'[24] Of course this is an over-simplification because Meguri is equating Club Méditerranée's brand of holiday making with vacationing per se. There are many Westerners who just want to go sightseeing too as opposed to the more communal, vigorous, extrovert type of holiday however well laid on à la Club Méditerranée. However Club Med has a vacation village in Phuket, Thailand and from 1987, one in Sapporo, Hokkaido which was developed by SCM Leisure Development Company Ltd as a joint venture.

A serious problem that the Japanese tourist operator has to contend with is the acute lack of seats on inland flights. Trains, *Shinkansen*, are extremely expensive (17,000 yen return ticket Osaka–Tokyo), often only a few thousand yen cheaper than flying. Flights are therefore often very difficult to book. If you want to return to Europe from Tokyo (Narita Airport) and live in Osaka, you will often be wait-listed for the inland flight weeks, even a month in advance, to leave the country; and then on the return flight have to pray on arrival at Narita that you will be given a flight back to Osaka. It is exceedingly frustrating. The best advice for anyone visiting Japan, who also has appointments outside Tokyo, is to enter and leave Japan from another airport. The additional charge of 2000–3000 yen levied on passengers leaving the country from Narita, 'for special services', is adding insult to injury. No doubt the real problem is shortage of airspace. More flights would lead to a repeat of congestion above as there already exists below on the roads.

Any tourist operator will have so many practical difficulties with which to contend. Moreover there will be local competition from The Japanese Travel Board (JTB) which has a very large share (some think a stranglehold) on the market. JTB offers a reasonably good but not always a particularly inspired or cheap service. But JTB has its own problems too, especially with foreign visitors who have a too romantic view of Japanese culture and find that local loos and mosquitoes tend to disturb it. Indeed the tourist industry must be one of the most frustrating for both sides of the counter.

Our concern here is not so much with the foreigner wanting to visit Japan, although one imagines that for the expatriate tour operator with local knowledge, there are great opportunities to present Japan to the world back home. Our concern is mainly with the Japanese who want to go abroad as a potential market for the foreign tour operator to enter. Everybody says this market has great potential as the Japanese are now starting to take annual vacations and want to see the world as never before. Now with the strong yen, they can well afford to do so.

Kondo Takashi of JETRO was insistent on the point that the Japanese need two things: more space and more recreational facilities: and, by implication, both are denied the average Japanese in their own country. This may seem absurd, but one concludes from this that the best way to sell to the Japanese, in this branch of commerce, is to get them out of Japan, that is to first export the domestic market customer. Thus you save yourself the trouble of actually going to Japan to compete on the domestic market – obviously absurd unless you, as a foreign tourist operator, are able to joint venture with a local one who obligingly sends you the customers.

This idea is definitely less ridiculous than it might at first sound, if only because many Japanese are already taking golfing and other activity holidays in Hawaii. They are interested in buying golf courses and opening clubs abroad. Golf is so limited and expensive at home. Young Japanese adore sport and it seems to me all forms of loud music. One would have thought that the scope for providing both, on package style holidays in Europe and America was unlimited, if properly organized and marketed. Again the great practical difficulty would be availability and the price of air tickets. Tickets sold in Japan are usually appreciably more expensive than those bought abroad. Many people fly to Hong Kong or elsewhere and buy the rest of their tickets there. However group tickets are relatively cheap to buy in Japan.

Moreover, when it actually comes to price, even young students, whom one would have thought do not have a great deal of money at their disposal, are prepared to pay vast sums to go abroad, so great is the desire to do so. But there must be a market to be tapped, if prices could be reduced somewhat for young people who, if satisfied, will surely come again and spend even more money. One imagines it is the young people who are going to change attitudes and thus ultimately open up domestic markets, but do not forget the ageing population.

Advertising

Advertising seems so much in the hands of local companies, especially Dentsu, that one imagines that to attempt to run an advertising venture in Japan would be doomed to failure from the start. Peter Cove of Cove–Ito Advertising Ltd, who formerly worked for a Japanese advertising company locally, started up his own agency with a Japanese colleague, Kazuhiro Ito, concentrating on Japanese export companies which included Nippon Steel and Honda. But they needed cash and had to borrow the money to pay a female employee her 60,000 yen bonus; went to celebrate with her (which used to be the custom in business) and had to borrow back half from her to pay the bill! They then took the right decision which was to tap the domestic market in an economy that was shifting from an export-driven economy to a domestic demand led economy. However they worked for foreign as well as Japanese companies and it was with BMW that they had their most eye-catching success. Cove said about working for Japanese companies that they 'are not willing to get outsiders involved with their planning because they do not want anyone to get close to their company secrets'.[25] He claims that 'companies have dominant powers over advertising agencies, and their relationships are not really professional'.[26] Interestingly too

Cove–Ito has 45 employees in its Tokyo head office with only two Japanese. Cove is however married to a Japanese. When Cove–Ito started in 1975 Cove believed that being small was a good thing because you could be more flexible than the large competitors. Now he feels that with increasing competition you either need the muscle of the big boys or, if you are to start up on your own, then you need the time and patience, above all to develop a group of people who are loyal to your agency philosophy.

Newspapers

The *Financial Times* has had a Tokyo liaison office since 1977 to sell advertising which comprises 80 per cent of total revenues. Forty-six per cent of this is earned in Japan – hence its importance. From June 1990 the FT has been printing in Tokyo. It is already printed in Frankfurt and France apart from London. The decision to print in Tokyo as well increases globalization of the newspaper. As local representative director, G Terence Damer, explains, 'Tokyo will become the Asia–Pacific center from which papers will be shipped to Asian and Oceanic Countries.'[27] Local manager Yoshinobu Miyashiro, paid tribute to the way head office gave Tokyo the power to make final decisions apparently right from the beginning when he and a secretary worked alone. Interestingly enough the FT published regional surveys of Japan and Miyashiro says, he has been 'thanked by local people for shedding light on their regions that even Japanese media are not interested in covering'.[28]

Harlequin, the publisher of romances *par excellence*, began business selling translations in Japan in 1979, but there was soon to be competition from a disgruntled North American distributor, with whom Harlequin no longer wanted to do business. The competitor arranged with Sanrio to publish Silhouette Romance books which adversely affected Harlequin's market. Harlequin bought the Silhouette copyrights and started publishing essays as well as selling a popular American board game in Japanese. However the real change for the better came when Takamasa Sago, who had previously worked 28 years for *Newsweek*, took over the Harlequin office and revamped Harlequin's image in Japan. He had the translation improved, shredded former titles when new ones came out and rewarded loyal and prolific Harlequin readers with attractive premiums of Royal Copenhagen china, flowers flown in from Holland and Schaeffer pens, including now a tie-up arrangement with Mikimoto (cultured) pearls. His premiums fitted the romantic world which he created in print for his readers. Sago also issued 'bunko' editions, that is special editions for sale in super-markets and at station kiosks. Harlequin's annual sales in Japan have passed 10 million copies. The moral of this success story is, once again, to have the right local man.

For those who want to enter the Japanese market, open an office and start selling immediately, there are foreign companies on the spot who specialize in providing help. They sell their *own* expertise at originally having settled in so successfully.

Helpmates International Group run by Z K Jaszai, a Hungarian who became an American citizen and worked for *The Japan Times*, says that foreign companies had difficulty in recruiting local staff because of the local life-time employment system. He helps foreign as well as Japanese companies. (45 per cent of clientele is foreign, 30 per cent Japanese, 25 per cent accounts for joint ventures.) His services even extend to setting up a distribution network. His philosophy is not to do in Rome what the Romans do, but something different, above all extra. You just have to be 'persistent, committed, and you've got to be very smart in your business,'[29] Jaszai advises. The trouble is, not everybody can be smart, but then, if they are not, he would argue, they should not try to enter the Japanese market.

Another agency is The Jardine Business Centre which conveniently advertises its services in *The Japan Times*. Such adverts in the local English language press are always welcome, as using a Japanese telephone directory can be *very* difficult. Of much use are *The Japan Times Directory* and the AT&T & NTT City Source English Telephone Directories which are sometimes given free with a new line.

The ability of a foreign company to introduce new commercial concepts is a yardstick of its success on the Japanese market. An example is Manpower Japan. A F J Finaty, who is company president, admits that strictly speaking his company, founded in 1966, legally, did not exist, indeed was not acting in accordance with the law which only allowed public labour exchanges to arrange for the supply of labour. At first most of his clients were foreign. But Manpower's success excited interest and later opposition from a local company which had been authorized to do the same type of business as an exception. This company then filed a suit against Manpower but the Prosecutor's Office rejected the suit and remarked that new legislation was needed. This followed in 1986. Finaty then joined an American franchised organization called Tokyo Manpower, but only on condition that he was given a free hand. He was and this worked to the advantage of both parties.

Significantly Finaty made a Japanese, Shozo Saito, national manager in 1968 so the professionalism of the company's work is very much a joint effort. Not only is care taken in the technical skills of Manpower employees hired out to other companies but in the attitude of those employees to their work, such as always being back 10 minutes ahead of time to begin their work.

A further second concept to get across to the Japanese markets was to upgrade the rôle of female employees not only in the minds of employers, who were expected to treat them properly, but also in the minds of the employees themselves by providing them with adequate training facilities.

Notes

1. JETRO International Communication Department (1990) *The Challenges of the Japanese Market. How 144 Foreign-affiliated Companies Succeeded*, (overview).
2. ibid, p3.
3. ibid, p4.
4. The problems (obstacles) experienced were 'Personnel recruitment', 'Fierce Competition', 'Business practices' and 'Distribution Networks'.
5. JETRO (1990) *Challenge 1*, (see Bibliography, p147) p11.
6. ibid, p20.
7. ibid, p22.
8. ibid, p37.
9. ibid, p47.
10. ibid, p73.
11. JETRO (1990) *Challenge 2*, (see Bibliography, p147) p2.
12. ibid, p8.
13. ibid, p9.
14. ibid, p40.
15. ibid, p60.
16. ibid, p9.
17. ibid, p11.
18. ibid, p11.
19. JETRO (1990) *Challenge 3*, (see Bibliography, p147) p35.
20. ibid, p39.
21. JETRO (1990) *Challenge 4*, (see Bibliography, p147) p11.
22. See Boye De Mente (1982) *The Tourist and Real Japan. How to avoid the Pitfalls and get the most out of your trip.* Tuttle, Tokyo: 10th printing, p42.
23. JETRO (1990) *Challenge 5*, (see Bibliography, p147) p8.
24. ibid, p17.
25. ibid, p19.
26. ibid, p19 (paraphrased).
27. ibid, p29.
28. ibid.
29. ibid, p36.

Part II

Doing Business with Japan Abroad

8

Japanese Business with the World

Is working (or doing business) with the Japanese abroad and working with them at home so different? In Japan the Japanese are on their own ground and foreigners have to conform in general to the Japanese way of doing things. Abroad the Japanese themselves have to conform or so one might think. Often the Japanese will have done their homework so well that the transformation for them may appear to be more effortless than it in fact was. Sony's Akio Morita's many initially failed attempts to enter the American markets show that considerable effort is required.[1] Foreigners entering the Japanese market at home have to be prepared to try equally hard. So much is obvious, even if it does at times tend to be forgotten by some impatient people. Successful as the Japanese are in smoothing out the difficulties, they experience sometimes cross-cultural clashes when trying to transfer Japanese management concepts abroad.

It is vital for the American economy to be able to have Japanese companies work smoothly, as long as they enhance the economy without putting local labour out of work, say in Detroit. To what extent it is the Japanese who are responsible for Detroit's problems is a matter for detailed study and is not initially our concern here.[2] What are the teething problems and long-term results of transferring Japanese management techniques?

Here we can test the potential for cross-cultural business harmony or otherwise, in doing business with the Japanese abroad. There have been a number of studies on labour in Japanese factories abroad. Joseph J Fucini and Suzy Fucini produced a study based on an American Mazda plant and called it appropriately *Working for the Japanese*.[3] The authors of this book explain the problems which American managers and workers had working for a Japanese company at different plants. While paying tribute to the efficiency of work and production procedures, they sometimes question the system's humanity. The book lists grievances and makes depressing reading, especially the battle between Mazda and the unions. However, towards the end of the book, the authors write: 'without studying a representative cross-section of plants run by the Japanese in detail, it would be impossible to draw sweeping conclusions about their treatment of workers.[4]

Stephanie Jones's *Working for the Japanese: Myths and Realities. British Perceptions*[5] gives a different picture based on a survey of British executives working for Japanese companies in England. This was exclusively a white collar study – whereas the Fucinis' was both but with the emphasis on blue collar. It would therefore be rash to attempt comparison of both Japanese management in America and England based on these two books alone; however Jones does try to distinguish between 'myths and reality' in regard to what has so often been heard about Japanese management.

The conclusion to be drawn from Jones's book is that even if the Japanese are clannish, exclusive in decision-making at home, workaholics and consensus-minded to a degree, in dealing with British managers in their UK companies they are not so – or so in such a way as to impinge upon good relations. Japanese management from an English, Western point of view, is acceptable. British executives noted the positive aspects of Japanese management: planning for the long term, hard work, life employment (job-security). Where the survey became interesting because it approached the controversial, was the reputation the Japanese apparently have for paying low salaries. In the past Japanese workers in Japan were seen as receiving low pay and the Japanese, when first in Britain, appeared to follow in this tradition. However, they have now moved to paying the full market rate, but apparently there are gripes from those working for smaller companies.

In the UK, a straight monthly salary is paid which includes the bonus (usually paid twice or four times a year in Japan). However notwithstanding this structural difference the total salary levels were considered to be low by British standards and Sir Peter Parker admitted that 'we have had difficulties in getting good sales staff and marketing people, and top quality personnel staff. So we pay our managers quite high in the UK.'[6] Where the Japanese are slow to improve salaries, staff leave, so they adapt. In Japan Jones argues, 'the Japanese seem comparatively underpaid, except for those in senior positions' and rightly concludes that 'although it is a myth that the Japanese pay low salaries, it is unlikely that they will ever be the most generous. Yet to many, the long-term security offered is worth much more than money in their pockets today.'[7]

As for working conditions, those in Japanese companies in England are comparable with those of other British companies, certainly seldom worse and often better than in Japan where space is always at a premium.

JAPAN AND THE USA

The Japanese relationship with the USA is often a tense one. It is also extremely complicated, spanning the past war and the present peace. America defeated Japan on the battlefield. Now the roles are reversed in the marketplace. Both need each other, Detroit Illinois (Chrysler) and Tokyo (Mitsubishi). Lee A Iacocca and Mitsubishi explicit in their jointly owned company, Diamond-Star Motors Corp in Illinois, have urged President Bush to limit the Japanese auto industry's market share in the USA. Furthermore he has accused Japan of 'selling products below cost', that is 'dumping'.

The question of dumping is a difficult one to define in terms of Japanese production processes, especially where Japanese wages are lower than American, unions are tamer and much work is performed by subcontractors at even lower wage rates. It must be very difficult to compute the true cost of a product.

Rice

In some areas of trade, such as rice, the American–Japanese debate over Japanese import barriers has the appearance of high farce, when American trade-fair officials are threatened with arrest at a local trade fair unless they remove exhibits of rice! Yet absurd as this was, there is no denying the complexity of the underlying political problem. The Japanese Liberal Party which is now in power is itself an uncertain alliance of competing factions, and only remains in power because of electoral support from the heavily overweighted rural areas which depend for their livelihood upon producing agricultural products, the main one being rice. Were the present government to open the domestic rice market to American imports, it would lose rural and thus electoral support and probably not survive the next general election.

As it is the government pays subsidies to rice growers which are unrealistically high and thus keep the price for the consumer artificially high as well. Historically rice was not a staple product but a luxury food which people could not afford to eat everyday and Japan was formerly an importer of rice, as it still is, although I gather that the matter is very complicated because of GATT negotiations. The Japanese make great play with the argument that as rice is a staple product, like bread for Westerners, the country has to be able to produce enough of its own in order not to be dependent upon imports from abroad. However, rice consumption is falling steadily as an increasing percentage of Japanese eat Western style.

For the Americans simply to demand that the Japanese open up the domestic rice market is not going to solve the Liberal Party's problem. One interesting development is an alteration in the tax levied on land sales (high land prices themselves being a thorn in the side of the Government). By reducing the level of tax for the sale of land for building, farmers thus have an inducement to reduce agriculture and profit from selling the land for building. Thus, presumably, their loyalty to the Government will not be weakened, at least in the short run. If however the number of new constituents are urban dwellers whose political sympathies lie elsewhere, then the rural vote itself will necessarily change. The problem then remains of how to satisfy the Americans and not sour the farmers on which the Government (the Liberal Party) has hitherto depended for its votes.

The rice debate, though it repeatedly hits the headlines because no doubt it appears to highlight Japanese intransigence so easily, is itself only one side of the coin of intransigence. The other is American. The Americans can be tough too.

The Big Stick – Super 301 Trade Law

The aim of this law is 'to penalize Japan's alleged unfair trade practices'.[8] Its success is muted because Japanese goods sell so well in the USA. So do American goods in Japan if they are of the right quality and price, and of course allowed in.

Collusion payments

The practice is at present that the US Government demands and obtains compensation from Japanese companies which rig prices and thus exclude foreign, in this case American, competition for contracts for work on the Japanese market. A case in point, reported in *The Daily Yomiuri* (12 May 1991, p12) was the price rig collusion of 11 local companies for telecommunication systems contracts at US Air Forces bases in Japan.[9] To the Americans this must surely have been adding insult to injury. However, cooperating on price is very much a local way of doing business and has at times been done under the auspices of MITI where the situation demanded it, so as to ensure fair shares for all. Keeping prices artificially high this way is perhaps another matter.

The Structural Impediments Initiative (SII)

The main problem, as far as the Americans are concerned, between the two countries in matters of trade are the so-called Japanese non-tariff barriers, often infrastructural and organizational. The aim of SII is to reduce and, where possible, remove them. It is a very sensitive series of issues dealing with many factors which the Japanese argue are their own affair and no true concern of America. However, because of their former post-war relationship with America and, above all, because they are dependent for their exports on keeping a large share of American markets, the Japanese continue to make concessions, gritting their teeth, as one feels, while doing so.

The Japanese feel that American troubles reflect poor industrial performance exacerbated by poor quality of products and high labour costs. They point to the many American companies which have a very profitable relationship with Japan. It is a never-ending debate. Undoubtedly there is right on both sides to the extent that the Japanese do have exclusionary practices and some American exporters, would-be importers, do have a quality and cost problem. Moreover, just as the Japanese resent Americans requiring reforms to the Japanese system which would benefit American importers, so do the Americans resent Japanese pointing out problems with the American economy. One could try and sum up a very complicated series of unresolvable problems by arguing that the Japanese are loath to reform unless it is seen to be in their own interest, while the Americans really only want to compete on equal terms or what they feel to be such. Both sides claim that the other is cross-culturally insensitive, the Americans about Japanese rice, the Japanese about American unions.

Reconciling differences

The absurd aspect about these negotiations, some observers think, is the fact that while there are apparently so many sources of disagreement between the two trading partners, there are so many joint ventures and interlocking operations which make a nonsense of the hysterical way Americans, such as Iacocca, castigate the Japanese while benefiting from working together with them. According to Shintaro Ishihara, Iacocca 'typifies that irresponsible breed of American executives who have become fabulously wealthy on the backs of American workers.[10]

Effect of recession

Meanwhile the recession (at the time of writing) casts its gloom upon the scene with Japanese automobile manufacturers agreeing on their own accord to limit exports to America simply because total sales there are declining. The question may well be asked whether the best corrector of the American trade deficit with Japan, is not just to let the recession reduce the balance itself. However this does not help the Japanese who do not want to have the Americans export their recession to the Japanese market which is itself already showing signs of strain with sliding land prices and production levels.

Anti-trust versus collusion

It is said that when the Japanese came to translate books on American trade laws and concepts into their own language, certain concepts proved difficult to accept. The concept of anti-trust was one of them. Americans often accuse the Japanese of collusion, that is agreeing on sharing market possibilities, even prices. This is anathema to the Americans. The Japanese find such views inconsistent with their own corporate way of thinking. Obviously they are not against competition but it is competition within limits.

Unitary tax

Whereas the Americans rail against Japanese tariff and non-tariff barriers or any form of discrimination against foreign imports or involvement in domestic markets, they do discriminate against foreign involvement in their markets too. One example of this is the 'unitary tax' which operates in some American states. Its effect is to base a foreign subsidiary's tax assessment not just on its business transacted in the state concerned, but worldwide too. Morita describes his efforts, partially successful, to have this tax rescinded as a member of the *Keidanren* delegation committee 'to investigate the investment situation based on the environment'[11] in 1984. American states are obviously caught between the advantages of encouraging direct Japanese investment, such as opening up factories on the one hand and the competition which such factories mean for local industry on the other.

JAPAN AND ASIA

The great temptation for Japan is to concentrate on Asia to the detriment of the West. Asian markets are nearer and easier to enter and to control. Japan towers over Asia economically in peace as it did in the past in war. Apart from Russia, Japan was the predominant power in Asia. It was really to preserve that predominance, especially over China, that Japan went to war with America. Japan and Britain could accommodate each other in Asia so long as there was no mutual interference. America was not prepared to be so accommodating. Now Japan has to accommodate China. One could say that the original aim of pre-war American diplomacy, to prop up China, has been achieved with a vengeance.

Economically speaking though, Japan is stronger in peace than it ever was before. All Asian countries are virtually economically dependent upon it although in some industries they are beginning to catch up (automobiles in South Korea, hi-tech in Singapore and Taiwan, food products in Thailand, and rattan furniture, together with a multitude of products, from Indonesia, one of the largest importers to Japan) because they can compete with cheaper labour but still not in technology. How long Japan can maintain the lead here must vary from industry to industry and be for some merely a question of time.

It is from the NICs (Newly Industrialized Countries) that the threat to Japan's world economic supremacy may come, not so much because of competing technical expertise, but cheaper labour. The Japanese manage to maintain a lead because of superior technology coupled with greater automation and investment in robots compared to that of their competitors. Japanese quality of manufactured products still enables them to surpass their rivals. However it is not just a question of competing with the NICs but also doing business with them. Here again Japanese imports remain at a high rate.

On the whole it seems unlikely that the NICs will swallow or supplant Japan. The Japanese are too clever for that and know how to use the extent of NICs' dependence upon Japan to divide and rule. One very important factor is Japan's political stability and industrial peace and discipline which no longer obtains in South Korea.

JAPAN AND RUSSIA

Japan looks longingly at the large virgin markets on the Russian continent and Russia covets Japanese capital and technical expertise. What holds things up as far as the Japanese are concerned is Russian reluctance to hand back the Northern Islands which Russia grabbed at the end of the last war immediately prior to the Japanese capitulation. The Russians adopted the same tactics when invading Manchuria which the Japanese had ruled as a colony wrested from China in the Sino–Japanese War (1937–1945). The Japanese put up no resistance; they were on the verge of surrender or had indeed already surrendered. The Russians took many Japanese prisoners and carted or marched them off to Siberian prison camps where many thousands died, many being held after the war had ended, though of course a peace treaty still has not been signed. *The Daily Yomiuri* (8 May 1991, p1) reported Michio Watanabe, former chairman of the Liberal Democratic Party Policy Research Council, on a visit to the Russian Republic leader Boris Yeltsin in Moscow as saying: 'before any large scale expansion of bilateral trade it was indispensable for the northern territorial issue to be solved and for Moscow to recognize that it had held Japanese prisoners of war in detention in Siberia long after World War II had ended. These issues are the causes of Japanese mistrust in the Soviet Union.'

Japanese resentment is still high. The recent visit by Gorbachev in

April 1991 went some way to assuage Japanese feeling (Gorbachev visited Japanese graves on Russian soil with suitable respect and lists of the formerly untraceable internees are being turned over to the Japanese authorities with expressions of regret). The one thing Yeltsin will do is hand back the Northern Islands, which he does not need either for strategic or economic reasons not without wringing as much financial assistance out of the Japanese as he can. The longer he holds onto them, he reckons, the higher the price the Japanese will pay for their return.

Russia's immediate problem is solving economic and political problems at home, the two being inextricably entwined. She desperately needs Japanese financial aid now which of course the Japanese will not give until the islands are returned. An immediate problem for Japanese exporters to Russia is her chronic shortage of foreign exchange reserves. While the larger companies can ride long periods of unpaid bills, the smaller ones cannot. The quicker the Northern Islands are returned, the sooner Russia will benefit from Japanese help. The recent deal on Japanese exports of Russian oil deposits should help.

JAPAN AND THE UNITED KINGDOM

Prince Charles and Margaret Thatcher have both been very enlightened in their dealings with Japan, the former got or was instrumental in obtaining Japanese investment in his principality, Wales, and the latter in creating a climate of understanding for the Japanese and satisfying them in such a way that was mutually beneficial. Of course the value of investment and trade between Japan and the UK is far less than that between Japan and America. Nonetheless the way Anglo–Japanese relations have been handled is instructive for all. World War II memories have lingered in the UK perhaps longer than elsewhere if only because Britain was in the last war longer and bore the brunt initially with greater severity.

It was the last war which really 'robbed' Britain of her empire, however many British people were keen to see this happen. Unlike America, one could say that the UK, while maintaining her honour, gained little from the war. Indeed she lost heavily economically. But possibly precisely because she did lose so much power and influence, she learnt greater sensitivity in dealing with a former enemy, now turned powerful friend, running an economy which is twice the size of Britain's and of immense importance to it. Mrs Thatcher may have been unimaginatively isolationist towards Europe, but her attitude towards Japan was a model of tact and understanding. Prince Charles nobly helped too.

This is not to deny that there have been difficulties, perhaps even some British protectionist reluctance initially to admit Japanese banks and security houses to the City of London. But such protectionism was not only reserved for the Japanese. The Americans too had their share of it. Indeed the cosy world of the City of London was, until the 'Big Bang', exclusive to a degree as far as the Stock Exchange was concerned. The opening up of the market to investment and securities houses was not an unmitigated blessing, as the series of fraudulent practices which occurred showed. The City had more than its own fair share of scandals.

It is very instructive to compare Japanese with British scandals; the British takeover in the style of Guinness, the Japanese securities and loan scandals. Neither, by definition, because of different institutional business structures, could have the same type of scandal. The ability to cheat seems to be the same. Neither side need be surprised nor criticize the other in this respect, save that in Japan scandals seem to be more institutional than personal. Sensibly neither indulges in a holier than thou altercation which seems sometimes to mark the American–Japanese debate on protectionist attitudes.

The UK is at the top of Japan's investment list for a number of important reasons:

1. The UK welcomes Japanese investment. Government is sensible and woos it.

2. The UK is a foothold in the EC, indeed offers a place for coordinating Single Market activities and an ambassador to inter-cede for understanding of Japanese aims. Japan has been very clever in obtaining badly needed British support and probably rues the day that Mrs Thatcher's sun set and Mme Cresson's rose!

3. The UK has an abundant supply of labour (relatively cheap and willing) and land available to set up manufacturing plants.

4. Japanese products are welcomed too, especially cars which are reliable, reasonably priced and well styled. Ditto electronic equipment.

5. The chemistry works between the two countries in spite of the war which possibly in the UK of all the countries of the Western world has been least forgotten. The Japanese were also greatly helped by the former ambassador, Kazuo Chiba, who, judging by his speeches, appears to be the soul of wit and understanding. British ambassadors seem on the whole more rarified and possibly, at least in the public image, less effective however much they may achieve behind the scenes.

Doing business with the Japanese in the UK requires equal understand-ing of Japanese culture because it is so juxtaposed with the local British variety.

Now that the British worker has himself become aware of the, sometimes self-defeating, efforts of the more fractious unionists, there is more understanding for Japanese management techniques which are dedicated to getting on with the job in a state of harmony, a state which aims to avoid all overt differences in status and privilege which so rankle British workers.

Japanese management is attuned to the needs and preference of British workers and sensibly does not try and force essentially Japanese practices upon them. No company song-singing early morning, no physical jerks mid-morning, but of course no slacking either – long tea breaks and so on, but appreciation for effort and loyalty shown in material terms.

Margaret Thatcher saw that Japan and Japanese mercantilism represented the true 'shot in the arm' which the British economy needed, more so than the Common Market with which she became increasingly disenchanted because of its costly semi-socialist, welfare state apparatus which she saw burdening the already overstretched British economy. She also remained sceptical about surrendering sovereignty, especially with the currency, to European control.

The Japanese offered, or seemed to be offering, a no-strings package deal: new factories in depressed areas mopping up unemployment, new management techniques to revive ineffective British ones. The Japanese were prepared to be conciliatory because the UK was the Trojan Horse for entry into the European market.

Both got or seemed to get what they wanted. As it has turned out the other EC members had discovered the Trojan Horse in their midst before nightfall and taken measures to limit Japanese access to the European market via the UK. Furthermore, in the UK the Japanese have revived depressed areas, mopped up some unemployment (they are basically labour savers), injected new ideas into British management, though possibly not enough as they have been extra sensitive to the cross-cultural difficulties involved (and not sought completely to Japanize local management). On the whole though it has been a success, but there is still a very long way to go. And, of course there are problems, for example the rupture between Nissan UK and Nissan Japan. But it is a success story. How successful and how significant, only time will tell.

Both the Japanese and the British are going to have to rethink their respective rôles. They may be faced with a far greater degree of cooperation than first envisaged, if neither can accommodate or be accommodated by the EC. This is the most interesting question of all. Britain still has its former colonial connections in trade. One sleeping giant, economically speaking, is Africa. South Africa has now obtained new respectability and has all the natural resources and raw materials at her disposal, of which Japan is denuded and desperately needs. China with its millions is another and Russia yet another. Were Japan to be repulsed in Europe and maintain her friendly connection with an equally dissatisfied UK, then the whole constellation of global economic power could be changed.

JAPAN AND THE EUROPEAN MARKET

One of the most difficult export problems to resolve is how to come to terms with the EC where customers appreciate, but manufacturers fear, Japanese imports. You could see the EC situation as a replica of the Japanese problem with foreign imports: customers are for, some local manufacturers are against. You could be nasty and say the Japanese are getting a taste of their own medicine at last. What complicates the issue is that the volume of Japanese imports is far greater than EC exports to Japan and, with some exceptions, EC exports to Japan are not as popular as Japanese exports to the EC. The Japanese have tried to show restraint by voluntarily reducing the volume of their exports, but this only exacerbates the problem of satisfying consumer demand while at the same time not being enough to placate local manufacturers.

The Europeans are however at one with the Japanese in the support they give to their own farmers which itself causes difficulties between members. The general EC problem is how to reduce subsidies. The German butter mountain ('Butterberg') is an example of where a subsidy helps farmers at the expense of the consumer and the Community as a whole. Japan does the same with rice. Having similar problems with agriculture should evoke mutual sympathy. The problems with cars, computers and electrical goods do not because, the EC claims, as do the Americans, that in effect the Japanese system of manufacturing allows and indeed demands low or relatively low prices which the EC, again like the USA, term dumping or near-dumping. In their terms, according to their manufacturing and pricing system, it is dumping for all practical purposes. The EC is even more mortified when the Japanese, using the UK as a manufacturing base, produce even more cheaply, utilizing full British tax concessions designed to attract Japanese manufacturers to the country. The EC contends that this is a form of subsidy which is contrary to its regulations.

The basic problem, as in the USA, is the excellence of Japanese products in comparison to local ones. This is the same problem that members of the EC, except possibly Germany, face when trying to increase exports to Japan. The quality of their goods, service and so on, does not always match that of Japanese products available on the home market. However where European products can compete in price, this is the one factor on the Japanese market, where consumers are used to paying high prices, which can inhibit sales when too low. Japanese consumers do not generally expect to pay low prices for European goods abroad. Quite the reverse is the case. One could say that part of the cachet of buying European is the high price tag. The price-conscious Japanese will not buy European goods but imports from Taiwan, China and South Korea. It seems absurd but perhaps the best thing the Europeans could do to capture the mass Japanese market would be to get the Japanese to re-export their imports into the EC back to Japan at European prices!

The Single European Market

Japan does not want to have to cope with a 'Fortress Europe' mentality, but sometimes has to because Japanese exports make such inroads into the EC and thereby threaten local industry. The European consumer buys Japanese because of price and quality. Often the home manufacturer cannot compete in both together. He also has difficulty, when so disposed, in exporting to Japan. There is little or no *quid pro quo*, hence EC tariffs and, to avoid them, Japanese voluntary export quotas. What irritates the EC exporter is the knowledge that Japanese imported goods into the European market are often not only cheaper but of better quality than those Japanese goods sold on the domestic market. The reason for this discrepancy is that cheaper prices in Europe are being subsidized by higher prices at home in Japan which irritates him even more. The European exporter cannot do tit for tat because the European consumer would not stand for it and of course would buy even more Japanese goods were this to happen. When the Europeans complain, as do the Americans for the same reasons, the Japanese often say the real causes for dissatisfaction are lack of real effort either to produce the right kind of goods to export to Japan or to deal with all the local problems involved.

This does not mollify the European who is manufacturing in a different situation to his Japanese competitors. It is a situation in Europe which he can alter to some extent, but not wholly. Europe is not Japan, but of course when the Japanese come to open factories in Europe, and in so doing prove that it is possible, even in Europe, to produce cheaply and with quality, the European is even less mollified. All he can then say is that Europeans are not Japanese. When the Japanese use local labour, local subcontractors, only have skeleton Japanese staff and still make a go of it, the European probably wishes either the Japanese would go home to Japan or that he himself could become Japanese!

Of course many over-simplifications are involved. Not every Japanese company can succeed in Europe and certainly not every type of industry. The Japanese concentrate on what produces and sells best. Not even the most fervent Japanese exporter or European fan would ever suggest that the Japanese bring their cumbersome distribution system over the water with them. As for living conditions, no one has yet suggested they should export their housing. Not everything exports. The Japanese exploit the gaps or create them. Europeans have to do the same, but, of course, it is not easy.

The European trump card and their attraction for the Japanese is the Single Market which suggests, though does not always mean, unity. Japan naturally is tempted to exploit disunity or, shall we say, reservations about full union as shown by the British. The key as well as the Trojan Horse for Japan is Britain. Presumably, too, Britain can use Japan to obtain better conditions. The danger is that in helping the Japanese to gain some possibly short-term advantage, Britain might weaken the Single Market ultimately to everyone's disadvantage.

JAPAN AND FRANCE

Akio Morita writing in his book *Made in Japan* appreciated the 1983 French 'Poitiers stunt'[12] as he calls it of requiring Japanese imports to pass through Poitiers and be individually examined by customs officials. After all Poitiers was where the French finally stopped the ancient Saracen invasion, but he explains that Japanese exports to France total US$1.9 billion and French to Japan US$1.2 billion. Japan can live without France, cognac and champagne, as well as antique furniture (yet not it would seem without other French luxury goods or their imitations!) but the French consumer is sold on Japanese electronics. Surely the main point is that the Japanese and French consumer want bilateral trade.

However, the French want equal opportunities to sell in Japan as they claim the Japanese have to sell in France – the old problem. Mme Cresson claimed that the disparaging remarks she made about Japan were not aimed at the Japanese as people, but at the Japanese conglomerates which, she felt, dehumanize the people, turning them into ants and thus enable the Japanese to swamp European markets. If this is what she believed or in fact said but was misreported before, then undoubtedly, apart from the unfortunate terminology used, Mme Cresson had a point. The Japanese are able to combine together and thus in matters of commerce and trade prove irresistible. Surely the next question for the French government is, should it just continue to complain or perhaps urge its countrymen to follow suit in some cross culturally acceptable way?

Not wanting to argue in terms of national clichés – French individualism versus Japanese solidarity – there is however an important sense in which mutual trade does involve a measure of cross-cultural understanding and behaviour. It was significantly at the height of the Cresson episode that a conference was held in Yokohama on Japan and the European Community and one of the local French business leaders present ended his speech by saying that in spite of everything, he remained 'optimistic'.[13]

What is so interesting about the Japanese 'French connection' is the plethora of French restaurants and patisseries in Japan. One would have to do a customer survey as to what extent customers reflect on the image of what they are buying, are drawn to particular tastes (cakes are often very Japanese!) or just buy from the corner bakery regardless of which national image is involved. The important point is surely that the French image is there at all, regardless of how much it is reflected upon by the Japanese consumer. At least it is something on which to build for the future. The Japanese do not have that same advantage in the catering trade in France. There are relatively few Japanese restaurants abroad. Surely the French could do more with the culinary foothold they already have in Japan.

JAPAN AND GERMANY

As with the 'French connection' in Japan, so the Japanese have a 'German connection' all too explicit in the restaurants, cafés and bakeries which bake and sell German cakes and bread. You find them everywhere in the plush *centre gais*, suburban restaurants, station bakery outlets and street cake shops. However, obviously it is in the motor car trade that the German connection is most visible on the streets or in the private garages of Japan.

The Germans, and we argue this elsewhere, seem much cleverer at cracking the Japanese market relatively speaking, because the volume of American imports is much higher (22.54 per cent of total foreign imports as opposed to 4.53 per cent German), but not significantly in cars where the Germans lead all other foreign importers. Japan import figures for 1991 show that in the classes 1000–1500cc, 1500–3000cc and 3000cc plus, German cars sold better than American cars, and in the latter two classes, better than any other importer. Only in the first class, 1000–1500cc were the Germans outsold and that was by the British. So why are the Germans so adept at cracking the Japanese market?[14]

Obviously, the BMWs, Mercedes, Porsches and, to a lesser extent Audis, appeal to the upper-income bracket consumer, or those who aspire to the status of belonging; Volkswagen to the less affluent. They appeal in quality of design, reliability and standard of local service and they have the extra cachet of being foreign and thus exclusive. They are not necessarily better, do not have to be better, than equivalent local products, they just have to avoid being appreciably inferior! However, they still have one great advantage over most equivalent American makes. They are the right size for Japanese roads – not too large or thirsty.

The Germans also seem to have the right marketing psychology.

They either make the distribution system work for them or set up their own. They also get the price right or arrange for suitable financing. BMW is an excellent example of this. Basically the Germans always seem to do their sums and planning right. They are very similar to the Japanese themselves in this respect. While writing this book, I have noticed how much better researched and comprehensive German specialist publications are. The great tragedy as far as Japanese–German commercial and other relationships are concerned is language: few Japanese speak German and even fewer Germans have mastered Japanese.

The crisis in their relations, if this is the correct term, is in the EC market, because hitherto Germany has dominated it and may have to surrender this position to the Japanese. The interesting question is whether, in spite of German involvement in the EC, she will not be prepared to curtail her operations there, if she is able to obtain special or even preferential treatment on the Japanese market. One can foresee that the solution to frustrations on the European market could ultimately be less profitable than greater involvement on the more lucrative Japanese market. It must surely be a great temptation.

AFRICA

The trouble with concentrating on growth, as opposed to Western-style profit-taking, is the constant search for new markets and the expansion of existing ones. You have to sell to get rid of the stuff, but of course only to those who can afford to pay. Black African states often cannot although Africa is still a vast market. South Africa remains the best market but until recently was in diplomatic quarantine. This made things very difficult for the Japanese as it did for the Americans, the British and the Germans, but all continued to sell in South Africa arguing of course that they were doing more for the blacks by continuing to trade with the country than by withdrawing. On balance, they probably were. Blacks have to work, eat and live. Even revolutionaries, unless supported from outside, need sustenance.

South Africa welcomed Japanese trade although it was still not always very diplomatic in how it treated the Japanese. A former Japanese Consul-General to Johannesburg managed to negotiate honorary white status for his countrymen but his daughter, who married a German professor, relates how when staying with her husband in a South African hotel, she had to occupy a separate bedroom.

Now South Africa is virtually free of sanctions, the Japanese are delighted to resume trade officially. They were upbraided by others for trading with South Africa at all. One absurd example was that I was not allowed to take my Toshiba Dynabook computer to South Africa on a writing holiday in 1990 because it was classified as being 'secret' as regards the South Africans. Nobody seems to have thought of the possibility of the South Africans, assuming they were interested, purchasing the computer elsewhere.

Notwithstanding the lifting of sanctions, there is apparently still a wait-and-see attitude on the part of some African companies or among each other: 'I'll wait till after you.' De Klerk's efforts for reform, which could lead to black rule or revolution if they are thwarted, do not necessarily promise stable economic conditions.

Notes

1. Morita, A with Reingold, E M and Shimomura, M (1990) *Akio Morita and Sony. Made in Japan*, Fontana, London, 3rd imp. (Especially chapter 'Selling to the World: My Learning Curve' and Morita's problems with American lawyers!)

2. See Kenichi Ohmai (1988), *Beyond National Borders* Kodansha, Tokyo and New York, p16: 'If Detroit wants to become internationally competitive (and not just with Japan), it must halve its work force and reduce pay by about 30 per cent.' Compare with Lee Iacocca's trenchantly expressed views on the matter. The point is of course that sacking 30 per cent of the work force may make sense economically but would be politically unacceptable. The Japanese could of course do this by cutting down on their part-time labour force and possibly rationalizing their subcontractors. What works in Japan would not necessarily work in America though it may be that some reconciliation between the two countries in this respect is ultimately going to have to occur. See Summary and Conclusion.

3. Fucini, J J and Fucini S (1990) *Working for the Japanese, Inside Mazda's Americanised Auto Plant*, The Free Press, Macmillan, New York and London.

4. ibid, p220.

5. Jones, S (1991) *Working for the Japanese: Myths and Realities. British Perceptions*, forewords by Sir Peter Parker and Haydn Abbott, Macmillan.

6. ibid, p102.

7. ibid, p107.

8. *The Daily Yomiuri*, 12 May, 1991, p8.

9. ibid, p12.

10. Shintaro, I *The Japan that can say No.* Simon & Schuster, New York, London, Tokyo, p82, see also p91. Compare with Iacocca on Japanese trade restrictions (*Talking Straight* (1989) pp188–9). He is very amusing.

11. Morita, A with Reingold, E M and Shimomura, M (1990) *Akio Morita and Sony. Made in Japan*, Fontana, London, 3rd imp, p306.

12. ibid, p261.

13. 'Je suis optimist.' (Conference: 'La Communauté Européenne' staged by the Institut France–Japonais at Yokohama 7–18 May, 1991 (Programme [Catalogue] 1991).

14. Japan Tariff Association (1991) *Japan Exports & Imports: Commodity by Country '91.12*, Ministry of Finance, Tokyo.

9

Japan and the Future

THE FUTURE

What of the future? Could it be war? George Friedman and Meredith
Lebard argue in the introduction to their recently published book with
its alarmist title, *The Coming War with Japan*, that

> there are underlying reasons – economic, political, and military – that must
> put the USA and Japan on a collision course. Essentially, the issues are the
> same as they were in 1941. Japan needs to control access to its mineral
> supplies in Southeast Asia and the Indian Ocean Basin and have an export
> market it can dominate politically. In order to do this, it must force the
> USA out of the western Pacific. The USA will see this attempt to force it
> out of the western Pacific as Japanese aggression and imperialism, as well
> as the desire to reduce the USA to the status of a second-class power. As
> in the 1930s, both will engage in a cold war against each other which will,
> in extremis, spill over into a hot war.[1]

While not wanting to comment on the military side of the problem,
undoubtedly it is the economic aspect which is at the heart of the
matter: Japan's insatiable demand for raw materials on which to base its
export drive to the USA; and the raw materials, especially oil, being in
effect under American control. If Japan became too commercially
tiresome and threatening, America could squeeze Japan dry. Whether
this could or ever would in fact happen is another matter. But if so, then
presumably anything could happen. The most interesting part of the
book, and by implication the most frightening, is the authors' analysis of
the Japanese economy. They argue that precisely 'the very factors that
helped create the modern Japanese miracle – the willingness of its
people to work hard, be frugal, and give their loyalty to their employer
and the state – threatens the growth of Japan's economy.[2] The authors
argue that restraint at home has meant having to transfer 'both
investment and consumption overseas'.[3] This in turn has led Japan to

try and offset its 'internal limits' by exploiting the rest of the world on which it has now 'become increasingly dependent . . . for its growth.'[4] The authors believe, and this is crucial to their military thinking, that

> since Japan's economy is more externally oriented than most, it will seek to correct the problems in its economy not so much by internal reform as by trying to take control of its external environment. This was Japan's solution during the 1930s, and it was not aberrant behavior on Japan's part. It followed logically from Japan's general condition, and that condition, controlled by geography more than by anything else, has not and cannot change.[5]

Where the argument seems to fall down is precisely in the question of economic power. Underestimating American economic power was the mistake made by both the Germans and the Japanese prior to the last war – the fact that they were not as powerful as the Americans economically. The Japanese economy is still only half the size of the American, it is dependent upon the American and no war could conceivably change this because ipso facto it could never be won. The Japanese realize this.

If, as the authors argue, America has a knife at Japan's throat, then the Japanese are surely not going to invite the Americans to use it. They would have to get rid of the knife first and to do that they would have to go to war which would be suicidal. Moreover there is no evidence to suggest that the Japanese are still militaristically inclined. Quite the reverse – ditto Germany. Both countries have learned their own lessons and concentrate on regaining their respective positions in economic terms. Of course, and it is one of the themes of this book, the Japanese are after world supremacy in trade – growth in world markets, especially the American where one-third of exports go, and this does cause considerable strain, is a form of conflict; but that all this should lead to war seems to us far-fetched. Surely you do not go to war with someone who accepts a third of your exports?

However the authors of *The Coming War with Japan* are right in drawing our attention to the seriousness of the problem in global terms. And I do believe, as argued above, that in a very real sense Japan is still at 'war', but it is not a military one and I most sincerely believe never will be either from the Japanese or from the American side. But, of course, accidents can occur and surrogate wars can be fought as they have been over oil and allied matters in the Middle East. Saddam Hussein may be Bush's bête noire now, but he was very useful to the latter's predecessors in office to keep the Iranians in check. There are flash-points in the Far East, but surely America and Japan, whatever their differences, and they are considerable, must realize that in the long run they have far more to gain through peace than war. And how could either side, indeed the whole world, survive such a war?

GLOBAL CHALLENGE

Ironically, one of the main problems Japan has is what to do politically with its new-found economic power whether Japan likes it or not. The impression given is that it would sometimes rather not be bothered because decision-taking can be so embarrassing and dangerous, for example in the recent Gulf crisis when Japan supported the Americans vocally, gave money moderately generously, but only sent mine sweepers to the area after the war was over. The spectre of war rekindles unpleasant memories of the past, unleashes old enmity between right and left, draws attention once more to the contradictions in the Japanese Constitution which forbids having armed forces although the country's Defence Force is one of the most powerful in the region.

After all Japan has been America's armed bastion in the Far East for some years now. Indeed it is America's perceived dependence upon Japan's military strategic position in the area which has enabled Japan to obtain so much preferential treatment from Washington, which turns a blind eye to Japan's inroads into the American economy. Japan's 'illegal' Defence Force is her greatest guarantor of continued high-level exports to the USA. American military needs, especially during the Korean War, were of course a great boost to the Japanese economy.

However, and this is of great importance for a highly sophisticated economy without oil as a basic natural resource, good relations with Arab oil suppliers is essential. Japan has to tread very carefully in the Middle East, especially in the Gulf, to do nothing which could remotely reduce the supply of oil or lead to the price being hiked too drastically. Of course this should have been a reason for Japan having immediately offered to help in the Gulf crisis. Then why did it not do so?

One very important reason could have been the Palestinian Liberation Organization's (PLO's) very shortsighted support of Iraq. There has been a whole saga of Arab, that is PLO, pressure upon Japan to disassociate itself from Israel. With such a cosy relationship between Saddam Hussein and Arafat in existence it might well have been that the latter did the former a favour by urging the Japanese to keep out of the conflict. At this stage it is pure speculation, but it would seem to make sense. Otherwise why should Japan which is so dependent upon Arab oil have been so embarrassed to support America which, so many people think, really went to war with Iraq to secure oil rather than just to liberate Kuwait? The only Arab group which consistently supported Hussein was the PLO, apart from Libya which could not have put any pressure upon Japan.

Japan is thus unwilling to assume global leadership because of its economic power, which when assumed, will endanger her economically. It would be self-defeating to do so. Japan will also do nothing or very little which requires armed intervention. It is however active in promoting peace and security in the region, especially in its hosting and presiding over Cambodian peace negotiations. Japan is a reluctant global leader and, with her history of possibly attempting too much, under-standably so. However in her slowness to react in the Gulf crisis, she disappointed, indeed angered, America and that is the last thing Japan wants or can afford to do. President Bush was very understanding this time. He or his successor may not be the next.

Notes

1. Friedman, G and Lebard, M (1991) *The Coming War with Japan*, St Martin's Press, New York.
2. ibid, p155.
3. ibid.
4. ibid.
5. ibid, pp156/157.

Summary and Conclusion

The ultimate global solution to economic problems connected with doing business with the Japanese is an agreement on mutual cross-cultural adjustment. The recent American–Japanese Structural Impediments talks are interesting and significant, not so much at the level they are held, but at a more profound level which the social changes (if American recommendations are adopted by the Japanese) imply. The discussions would be of far greater value if the Japanese were allowed to conduct similar discussions in the USA on the structural impediments to American business! Americans who want to change the nature of Japanese society also need to look at their own.

It is true many Japanese live in sub-standard housing, many without mains drainage or proper sanitation. But how many Americans are homeless, even semi-starving and, let's face it, on 'their beam ends'? It is well over a million, perhaps not such a large percentage of the total population, but growing all the time. In Japan the same people are virtually non-existent. While the Japanese way of doing things is by no means perfect, nor is the American or Western way either. Surely we ought not to forget that in trying to understand the Japanese, we tend, as happens in a number of books, to sit in judgement on them.

Obviously much that works in Japan would not work elsewhere in the West, but undoubtedly some of it would and of course does already. Perhaps there is a need for a little more Japanese austerity and discipline, work ethic (call it what you will) not as an antidote to Western hedonism, but simply because our system does not seem to work any more when in competition with theirs. Some adjustment would therefore appear to be called for. We in the West have had everything 'on a plate' for centuries. Now the plate is leaving our hands. The story of West and East has often been one between the haves and have-nots. Now things are changing. The West is played out economically in many respects, especially in regard to economic growth, when compared to rising Asian economies, not just in Japan, but Taiwan, South Korea,

Singapore, even Indonesia. The reader who reads this with a smile, possibly disdainful or superior, simply has to go to Japan and see how things are changing, how the Japanese can make anything we can, often better. They still have tremendous disadvantages, geographical, climatic and demographic, but their extraordinary ability to triumph is something we might consider seeking to emulate. And this we can surely never do without certain cultural adjustment.

MUTUAL UNDERSTANDING

Just as the Japanese go to great lengths to learn about Western culture, we will have to do the same and learn about theirs. Otherwise the problem of doing business with them will become correspondingly greater.

A Polish teacher (a great burly fellow), whom I met at a conference on cross-cultural interaction, had married a Japanese woman. He told me about the initial difficulties he had in winning over her parents and how he had ultimately succeeded and how he had assimilated much Japanese culture during his marriage (now blessed with children).

He explained too how it was the custom in Japan to take the gynaecologist a sort of premium payment after safe delivery of the child, which he refused to do. Instead he took along a generous supply of Polish cakes which he had baked himself. Doctors and hospital staff were delighted and on subsequent visits always remembered the cakes. What impressed me most was how he ended the story:

'Of course I've become partly Japanese too. I join in festivals' (indeed in the village where he lived his part in them had become an integral one). 'When I hear the (temple) bell, I'm off down there. There's no holding me.'

I felt he had culturally assimilated while maintaining his own Polish identity (the cakes) but at the same time had had the good sense and obvious joy of identifying himself with Japanese culture.

'What will the neighbours say?' his future in-laws had asked him at the beginning, trying to warn him off marrying their daughter.

'Just what you tell them!' he so wisely replied. And, by all accounts, they sensibly chose to tell the neighbours the truth; and the neighbours seemed equally wise to have accepted it.

Sandy Taubenkimel is another example of cultural conscience. He is an American Jew who was headhunted by a talent scout, introduced to a large American corporation, and interviewed with ease, until it was realized to what race Sandy belonged. The personnel director put his arm affectionately round Sandy and said the name Taubenkimel would not fit in with Smith and Brown. Sandy did business with the Japanese from California, then came over and started up his own firm. His first wife had died. He married a Japanese, younger than himself and they now have a daughter.

They speak mostly Japanese to each other. Sandy started off as an all-American American. Then he found himself giving up his car and cycling along the narrow streets with his wife. He had got used to sleeping on *tatami* in a *futon*, but pined for a king-sized bed. Ultimately he convinced his wife whom, Sandy says, is petite ('You can put her in your pocket') and bought an enormous bed for 80,000 yen and was proud of it. But somehow his wife, who no doubt was impressed at first, later became less so. Sandy found himself having to sell the bed for 30,000 yen and sleep in the *futon* on *tatami* once more. The only change he has succeeded in making is buying a small car and, so he imagines, convincing his wife that it is a better form of transport than a bicycle.

Sandy is President of the local International Business Association, which he took over with a 7,000 yen debt, now converted to a 2 million yen credit. He is still very American, proud of his country, but horrified at the increasing drugs abuse and the attendant social problems. He marvels at Japanese commercial and industrial prowess, thinking that at some stage Americans will have to roll up their sleeves and get down to work again. He is constantly aware of the difference between his American and his newly adopted Japanese culture. He wants to write a book entitled 'Japan, the country without a middle' by which he means that there is no halfway house between the local cultural opposites, the pre- and post-industrialism, the scandals and reforms, the old and the new.

Being president of this and governor of that, Sandy has become a local celebrity with his picture often appearing in the newspapers. Does that impress his wife, he asked her? No, not really, he is told, because she knows he is the most important *gaijin* (foreigner) in Japan. Sandy says he cannot commit himself to staying in Japan for the rest of his life. I think he already has.

The cross-cultural assimilation is not all one-sided. The Japanese do try with varying degrees of success to learn Western languages and customs, mainly American and English. How hard do we try to learn theirs? It always amazes me how Western businessmen expect to do business long term in Japan without learning the language, though many compromise (as stated above) by marrying a Japanese. But even then and however amazingly hard the Japanese language, any expatriate businessman has got to grit his teeth and learn it. Equally of course the Japanese are well advised to improve their antiquated method of teaching foreigners their language.

Mme Cresson's reference to the Japanese as yellow ants, though an insult and undoubtedly meant as such, evokes a picture of a live phenomenon which is irresistible, small in its minute individual living organisms, but at the same time of immense communal strength;

tireless and, this is the point, being everywhere – all-enveloping. Undoubtedly this points to profound truths about Japanese tactics which evolve from the structure of their society and resultant business culture.

The Japanese are everywhere all the time and this is their method, how they obtain growth and so increase their share of markets. They themselves are subject to dictates and the irresistible forces of their own system which relentlessly demand an increasing search for new markets to absorb increased units of production always being turned, even churned out, with increasing perfection and speed.

What appears sinister to others is their ability, by their very excellence, to swamp and drive out competition. The question one asks is what would happen, even if one can or could compete? The answer is, the Japanese would simply change course and go marching on in a different direction and in producing something else, but not necessarily to our advantage!

It has to be remembered that Japanese business, because it is to a great extent employee- and less shareholder-orientated, growth and less profit, the social consequences of competition from outside, gives a deeper significance for Japanese companies. Everyone sticks together and unites against the foreigner, who threatens such existence, and it is felt that there is nothing wrong in so doing, however nefarious some of the methods employed. For the Japanese it comes down to survival or extinction not just for the companies concerned but for all the closely connected network of interlocking groups. Far greater sensitivity is shown in personnel problems. The mass and highly insensitive redundancies recently carried out in the British publishing world would be unthinkable in Japan. I think we Westerners have got to start thinking more of each other in commercial and social terms and less of ourselves socially and solely in terms of profit. Or we have to plan and coordinate things much better to cushion the shocks among the community. We call ourselves Christian but do not on occasion appear to act that way. We have our own problem of illusion and reality. This is *not* meant to be a sermon, merely an attempt to follow Japanese lines of thought and thus be the better able to do business in the country, to which one has to be fully committed. I have never come across a successful expatriate businessperson who was not that.

Ultimately it will depend upon whether Japan becomes more lax, and the West (America, especially, and Europe) more productive; whether Japan moves forward to adopt more generous Western lifestyles, and the West makes do with more frugal ones; Japan completes her industrial revolution and ends feudalism, the West regains, without social regression, some degree of its former pioneering spirit and achievement. The present controversy as to whether Japan will converge on Western business practices or essentially continue to diverge from them, can surely not be resolved by Japan alone, but by Japan and the West. Japan does respond to pressure from abroad to open up her markets. However it is up to the West to offer the Japanese consumer what he or she wants. The question is: can the West do that? Can 'Talking Straight'-Iacocca produce cars not only Americans want, but Japanese too?

Sweeping away all the non-tariff barriers in Japan will not sell a single car, unless Mr and Mrs Yamada give up their idea of buying a local make. If the Yamadas want to buy American, they will. Young Master Yamada certainly will buy an Apple Computer if the price is right. He is already sold on its quality, and (significantly enough) 'user friendliness'. Surely it is this degree of imaginative skill which alone can capture Japanese markets. Excellence, in whatever form and product, will succeed. Japan bashing will not. And above all we are going to have to learn to speak each other's language in all senses of the word.

Useful Phrases

First, for communication, please realize that Japanese is to a very great extent an unspoken language. It is thus rich in gesture and silence.

Hara means belly and *haragei* is 'belly' – or gut-reaction – talk', that is essentially non-verbal communication between Japanese people which is often difficult for the foreigner to understand. It is not the words, but the meaning behind the words, which is significant. Of course this happens in other languages too, however the Japanese would appear to have developed it to a fine art.

I always like watching women talking to each other on the train. The one talks, the other nods without necessarily contributing any words to the conversation but the nodding is obviously very important. It is the most extraordinary procedure to watch. I imagine the nods express a basic sympathy between the two and are of a profounder significance than the words. The extraordinary ability a Japanese will have of keeping his or her end up in a conversation by merely using the filler *Ah, sodesuka?* and sometimes even that is reduced to a quick succession of *so, so* repeated at intervals. It gives the appearance of being a very elliptical method of communication. There is a lot of ellipsis in conversation which is regarded as still correct speech. I get the impression too that in the written language, once one has established what the grammatical subject as well as the topic are, then one can reduce the number of words. The fact too that words are written or rather drawn in kanji, the old Chinese script, also makes words in our Western sense more signs than words. The concision achieved is remarkable. Certainly the Japanese do not seem to waste words, indeed, through natural personal modesty, often seem to be at a loss for them. (See Matsumoto, 1988.)

'Yes' (*hai*) does *not* mean agreement, merely having understood. You judge agreement from the situation: if it is something simple, like a ticket, hotel room and so on, whether in fact there is an indication of getting what you want, the railway ticket, hotel room key, whatever. Always make quite sure. With business negotiations there is a whole art of learning whether the answer is 'Yes', but it may take some time to find this out and you will need a Japanese to interpret the signs for you.

'No' (*iie*) is seldom said. Instead you hear *dame* – it is not possible – or, much more likely you hear a long sentence, which you cannot understand, save for the crucial words *nai'n desu* which seems to mean ('there isn't any') or words to that effect. Or the other person will make a gesture of crossing his or her two index fingers, which is not very polite, but means 'definitely no!' It is often used with foreigners who cannot understand any Japanese. The much politer way and one that you will more often experience (and which you should practise) is the slow shake of the head with a mournful facial expression to go with it and a sound of an intake of breath. This means 'terribly sorry, but "No!"' (it's difficult, that is impossible) or stronger still *muzukaskii desu*. (The 'u' in *desu* is virtually a mute vowel.)

If you can understand the basics of 'Yes' and 'No', then you have understood the basics of Japanese. Confusion on these points leads to most verbal cross-cultural misunderstanding.

I find the best form of communication is to smile frequently, a warm friendly, but not over friendly, smile with which to overcome the almost certain possibility that the Japanese with whom you are communicating in English, force majeure, understands at the most 10 per cent of what you are painstakingly saying. The other person may smile, shake his or her head, and appear to have understood, even assure you of the fact, but you will find out later that this was not the case. Above all be prepared to explain something important at least five times. Pack into that vital 10 per cent range of listening comprehension only the basics of what you want in the simplest of language. Cut out all unnecessary words, however grammatically necessary. It is meaning you are after. No puns, no jokes, no being clever, just concentrate on making yourself understood. The rôles will be reversed when both of you have to rely on your Japanese!

Again 10 per cent will be understood. Therefore pack into that 10 per cent the basics of what you want to say. Go for the subject, that is the topic (what you want) first, and put that at the beginning.

Kohii o kudasai. (May I have a cup of coffee please.)

Kohii is coffee, *o* is object particle, and *kudasai* is asking nicely. The *o kudasai* is very useful because you can stick anything you want in front of it.

If you want to ask someone a question, then preface it with *Sumimasen* (excuse me) and then ask for what you want.

Sumimasen, Takushi (pronounced like taxi) *wa* (it's a particle meaning 'as for' indicating the topic), *doko desuka?* Where's a taxi?

Thanking someone is easy. Just say: *Domo arigato*, bow and smile. The bowing is the most important gesture of all. Do not overdo it, but obviously the more grateful you are or the more you want something, the deeper you go, but not too low. What is difficult is to combine status with desire. It is ridiculous to bow too low to someone younger than yourself or someone who is of lower situational status (this is not meant snobbishly), but if you desperately want something, you can, as a foreigner, well afford to go a bit lower.

Domo arigato
Doitashimashite (don't mention it)

Now for the simple greetings:

Ohayo gozaimusu	good morning
Konnichi wa	good afternoon
Konban wa	good evening
Oyasumi nasai	good night
Osakini-dozo	after you
Hajimemashite	how do you do!
Dozo yoroshiku	(literally, please, oblige)
Gomen-nasai	Excuse me. May I come in?
Ikura desu ka	How much?

In restaurants, where the waitress or waiter does not speak English and most of them know the vital words, ask for the menu, if there is one, and ask for a *setto* which is usually a two- or three-course meal reasonably priced – some menus have pretty pictures. Coffee or tea or a cool drink may be thrown in too. If it is early or before 11am, then ask for *morning* which is a cut-price breakfast, sometimes jolly good with egg, toast, coffee. Even if you have already had breakfast, have another one and save on lunch or *lunchi*, as it is called. Again *lunchi* is often another special deal with a two- or three-course menu. Go for it. Even some otherwise quite expensive restaurants ((and what is not expensive in Japan?) have very cheap *lunchi* menus or *settos*.

If it is in the afternoon, then order *cake setto* which again is a special deal with coffee and a piece of cake. If it is in the evening and you are foxed by the menu, are feeling tired and monosyllabic yet still very hungry, but feeling stingy, then either order 'curry rice' which will be affordable and fairly filling or 'chicken' which often is a 'setto' with soup (lovely miso [bean] soup and the inevitable chicken in some guise or other). It always tastes delicious and I have eaten it for several months while learning the language.

You will not starve if you have got the basics of communication. And you will save a fortune. Remember: *morningu* for breakfast or elevenses, *lunchi* for lunch, *cake setto* for afternoon tea and *curry rice* or *chicken* for dinner. Those are the really useful phrases.

The rest you can get from a phrase book. But I recommend one with an audio cassette. You will often hear everyone saying *Ah sodesuka?* which means roughly 'Is that so?' 'Really!' Practise saying it for all you are worth. But do not do what I did, pronounce the 's' in sodesuka like a 'z'. It then means 'Oh, that's an elephant!' German speakers (I speak a little), please beware. It took me a long time to realize, and then I had to be told, why everyone looked very puzzled or was convulsed when I tried to get round the language problem by using this otherwise invaluable filler. Others are *eto* (a hesitant 'I'm not sure'), sometimes reduced to an interrogative *ee* accompanied by a vacant (vacuous) look. Simple hesitancy in making a point in a discussion or when disturbing someone apologetically is to say *ano* and look suitably contrite.

If you want to speak Japanese, then *ganbatte* (keep trying). It is no different with the language, than it is with *Doing Business with the Japanese*!

Bibliography

By no means complete, the following lists grouped, roughly according to content, should provide a student of Japanese business and business culture with a basic library. I have aimed for books which offer information, practical help and above all the atmosphere and 'flavour' of the country. But I always feel the one great problem of books about Japan is that for us they have to be in our own language and not in Japanese. There must in my opinion always be an element of distortion in trying to explain Japan in Western terms. Given that reservation, you will get much more out of the books by continually questioning the conclusions their authors draw. Nothing is Gospel!

BUSINESS

Adams, T F M and Kobayashi, N (1974) *The World of Japanese Business*, Kodansha, Tokyo and New York.

Alletzhauser, A (1991) *The House of Nomura: The Inside Story of the World's most powerful Company*, Bloomsbury, London.

Alston, J P (1990) *The Intelligent Businessman's Guide to Japan*, Tuttle, Tokyo.

Anglo–Japanese Economic Institute (1989) *Doing Business with Japan: Case Studies and Analysis of British Success*, London.

Booz, Allen and Hamilton Inc (1987) *Direct Foreign Investment in Japan: The Challenge for Foreign Firms. A Study for the American Chamber of Commerce in Japan, the Council of the European Business Community*, Tokyo (1987).

British Chamber of Commerce in Japan (1987) *Research & Development in Japan*, Tokyo.

British Chamber of Commerce in Japan (1989) *Investing in Japan: Pointers from British experience*, Tokyo.

British Chamber of Commerce in Japan (1990) *Japan Posting: Preparing to Live in Japan*, Tokyo.

British Chamber of Commerce in Japan (1991) *Human Resources in Japan: Strategies for Success*, Tokyo.

British Chamber of Commerce in Japan (1991) *BCCJ 1991–92 Directory of Members*, Tokyo.

(The above five publications are available from the Department of Trade and Industry in London, P & B UK Ltd Japan Posting: Preparing to Live in Japan, Tokyo.

British Chamber of Commerce in Japan (1989) *Investing in Japan: Pointers from British experience*, Tokyo.

(The above four publications are available from the Department of Trade and Industry in London, P & B OK Ltd in the UK and the Japan Association. They are also available direct from The British Chamber of Commerce in Japan, 16 Kowa Building, 1-9-20 Akasaka, Minato-ku, Tokyo 107. Tel: (03) 3505-1734; Fax: (03) 3505-2680.)

Burstein, D (1990) *YEN! Japan's New Financial Empire and Its Threat to America*, Fawcett Colombine, New York.

Christopher, R C (1987) *Second to None. American Companies in Japan*, Tuttle, Tokyo.

Clark, R (1988) *The Japanese Company*, Tuttle, Tokyo.

De Mente, B (1989) *Business Guide to Japan: Opening Doors . . . and Closing Deals!* Yenbooks, Tuttle, Tokyo.

Department for Enterprise (1988) *Getting it Right in Japan*, a report on the proceedings of a seminar organized jointly by the CBI and the Opportunity Japan Campaign and sponsored by National Westminster Bank at Nat West Hall, London, on 13 December 1988.

Doi, T (1981) *The Anatomy of Self: The Individual Versus Society*, Translated by John Bester, Kodansha, Tokyo & New York.

Dudley, J W (1990) *1992: Strategies for a Single Market*, Kogan Page and Chartered Institute of Management Accountants, London. Also published as *1992: Understanding the New European Market* (1991), Dearborn Financial Publishing Chicago, Ill.

Fields, G (1989) *The Japanese Market Culture*, The Japan Times, Tokyo, 2nd edn.

Friedman, G and Lebard, M (1991) *The Coming War with Japan*, St Martin's Press, New York.

Frost, E L (1989) *For Richer, For Poorer: The New US – Japan Relationship*, Tuttle, Tokyo.

Fucini, J J and Fucini, S (1990) *Working for the Japanese: Inside Mazda's American Auto Plant*, The Free Press (Macmillan), New York and Collier Macmillan, London.

Gibney, F (1982) *Miracle by Design: The Real Reasons Behind Japan's Economic Success*, Times Books, (Quadrangle) New York Times Co, New York.

—— (1988) *Japan: The Fragile Super Power*. Tuttle, Tokyo, 2nd revised edn.

Horsley, W and Buckley, R (1991) *Nippon: New Superpower. Japan since 1945*, BBC Books, London.

Huddleston, J N (1991) *Gaijin Kaisha: Running a Foreign Business in Japan*, Tuttle, Tokyo.

Iacocca, L with Sonny Kleinfield (1989) *Talking Straight*, Bantam, New York.

JETRO (1982) *Now in Japan* (Nr. 33/1982. Ausländische Unternehmen in Japan, Tokyo.

—— (1983) Business Information Series 8: *The Tokyo Capital Market – Development and Prospects*, Tokyo.

—— (1983) Marketing Series 1: *Japan as an Export Market*, Tokyo.

—— (1983) Marketing Series 2: *The Role of Trading Companies in International Commerce*, Tokyo.

—— (1983) Marketing Series 6: *The Japanese Consumer*, Tokyo.

—— (1988) Marketing Series 8: *Doing Business in Japan*, Tokyo.

—— (1985) Business Information Series 11: *Investing in Japan*, Tokyo.

—— (1989) Business Information Series 12: *Labor Management in Japan*, Tokyo.

—— (1989) *Setting up a Business in Japan: A Guide for Foreign Businessmen* (Question and Answer), Tokyo.

—— (1989) *A Survey on Successful Cases of Foreign-affiliated Companies in Japan*, conducted by the Institute for Social Engineering, Inc, in cooperation with the Ministry of International Trade and Industry, Tokyo.

—— 1990 JETRO White Paper on Foreign Direct Investment. 'Expanding Global Investment Exchange and Japan's Responsibilities – Summary', Tokyo.

—— (1989) *1992 EC*, Tokyo.

—— (1990) *The Challenge of the Japanese Market: How 144 Foreign-affiliated Companies Succeeded*, Tokyo. There are six soft-covered, A4-sized volumes: *Overview*, then for convenience when writing this book privately numbered for reference: *Challenge, 1: Industrial Machinery and Parts, Computers and Software, Electric and Electronic Appliances, Automobiles, Ferrous and Non-Ferrous Metals*
Challenge, 2: Foods, Food Services
Challenge, 3: Consumer Goods
Challenge, 4: Chemicals and Pharmaceuticals, Medical Supplies, Oil Products, Rubber, Glass, Textiles, Paper Products
Challenge 5: Commerce, Communications, Newspapers, Publishing, Services.

—— (1990) Import Promotion Department, Tokyo:
STEP (The Business Person's Guide to the Japanese Market);
The Japanese Market Continues to Open up;

Who to Contact About Imports at Major Japanese Corporations. Entry points: a directory of Japanese Importers;
The Facts and Figures of Doing Business with Japan. The market: an introduction to Japan and sources of information;
Items Covered by Tariff Elimination and Tax Incentive Programs. Products subject to tariff elimination and tax incentive programs.

—— (1990) *The Japanese Market: A Compendium of Information for the Prospective Exporter*, Tokyo.

—— (1990) *The Business Person's Guide to Japanese Import Promotion: Items covered by Tariff Elimination and Tax Incentive Programs*, Tokyo.

—— (1991) *A Wealth of Opportunity: Distribution in Japan*, Tokyo.

—— (1991) *Nippon 1991 Business Facts and Figures*, Tokyo.

Johnson, C (1987) *MITI and the Japanese Miracle. The Growth of Industrial Policy, 1925–1975*, Tuttle, Tokyo.

Jones, S (1991) *Working for the Japanese: Myths and Realities. British Perceptions*, forewords by Sir Peter Parker and Haydn Abbott, Macmillan, London.

Jung, H F (1988) *How to Do Business with the Japanese. Told from Practical Experience*, The Japan Times, Tokyo.

Kahn, H and Pepper, T (1982) *The Japanese Challenge. The Success and Failure of Economic Success*, Tuttle, Tokyo.

Kang, T W (1991) *GAISHI. The Foreign Company in Japan*, Tuttle, Tokyo.

Katzenstein, G (1991) *Funny Business. An Outsider's Year in Japan*, Paladin, Grafton Books, London.

Keizai Koho Center (1991) *Japan 1991: An International Comparison*, Japan Institute for Social and Economic Affairs, Tokyo.

—— (1992) *Japan 1992: An International Comparison*, Japan Institute for Social and Economic Affairs, Tokyo.

Kenrick, D (1988) *Where Communism Works. The Success of Competitive Communism in Japan*, Tuttle, Tokyo.

Kojima, K (1984) *Japan and a New World Economic Order*, Tuttle, Tokyo.

Koren, L (1988) (illustration by Shack Mihara, research by Ziggie Kato) '283 Useful Ideas from Japan', *The Japan Times*, Tokyo.

—— (1990) 'Success stories: How eleven of Japan's most interesting businesses came to be', *The Japan Times*, Tokyo.

Krisher, B (1989) *Japan As We Lived It: Can East and West ever Meet?* Yohan, Tokyo.

Lagano, D (1989) *How to Make Money in Japan*, Yohan, Tokyo.

Lu, J D (1989) *Inside Corporate Japan: The Art of Fumble-Free Management*, Tuttle, Tokyo.

March, R M (1990) *The Japanese Negotiator: Subtlety and Strategy Beyond Western Logic*, Kodansha, Tokyo.

Miyazaki, I (1990) *The Japanese Economy: What Makes it Tick*, translated by Simul International, Simul Press, Tokyo.

Morita, A with Reingold, E M and Shimomura, M (1990) *Made in Japan: Akio Morita and Sony*, Fontana/Collins, London, 3rd imp.

Murray, G (1991) *Synergy: Japanese Companies in Britain*, PHP Institute Inc, Tokyo and New York.

NHK (1987) *Handbook for Film Anatomy of Japan. The Wellsprings of Economic Power*, with Introduction by Christopher, R C, Tokyo.

Ohmae, K (1988) *Beyond National Borders: Reflections on Japan and the World*, Kodansha, Tokyo and New York.

—— (1990) *The Borderless World: Power and Strategy in the Interlinked Economy*, Harper, New York.

—— (1985) *Triad Power: The Coming Shape of Global Competition*. The Free Press (Macmillan), New York and Collier Macmillan, London.

Okita, S (1990) 'Approaching the 21st Century: Japan's Rôle', *The Japan Times*, Tokyo.

Osaka Chamber of Commerce and Industry (1990) *Major Projects and Events in Osaka and the Kansai*, Osaka.

—— (1989) *100 Topics on Osaka*, Osaka.

Pascale, R, Tanner and Athos, A, G (1986) *The Art of Japanese Management*, introduction by Sir Peter Parker, Penguin, London.

Pinder, J (1991) *European Community: The Building of a Union*, Opus, Oxford University Press.

Prestowitz, C V (1989) *Trading Places: How America Allowed Japan to Take the Lead*, Tuttle, Tokyo.

Rebischung, J (1980) *Japan: The Facts of Modern Business and Social Life*, Tuttle, Tokyo.

Reischauer, E O and Craig, A M (1986) *Japan Tradition and Transformation*, Tuttle, Tokyo.

Roth, M (1989) *Making Money in Japanese Stocks*, Tuttle, Tokyo.

Sanders, S (1977) *Honda: The Man and his Machines*, Tuttle, Tokyo.

Saso, M (1990) *Women in the Japanese Workplace*, foreword by Ronald Dore, Hilary Shipman, London.

Seward, J (1987) *America and Japan: The Twain Meet*, Yohan, Tokyo, revised edn.

—— and Van Zandt, H (1987) *Japan: The Hungry Guest (Japanese Business Ethics vs. Those of the US)*, revised edn, Yohan, Tokyo.

Shintaro, I (1991) *The Japan that can say No*, translated by Frank Baldwin, foreword by Ezra F Vogel, Simon and Schuster, New York and London, Tokyo.

Sinha, R (1983) *Japan's Options for the 1980s*, Tuttle, Tokyo.

Suzuki, Y (1991) *Japanese Management Structures, 1920–80*, Macmillan, London.

Tadanobu, T, translated by Yoshinori Oiwa (1985) *The Japanese Brain*, Taishukan, Tokyo.

Taking on Japan (1988) *How 18 Foreign Companies Compete in the World's Second Largest Market*, Look Japan Ltd, 2nd edn, Tokyo.

Tanaka, H William and Takashima, Nobuyuki (1986) *Doing Business with Japan*, Business Books International New Canaan, Connecticut, USA.

Thian, H (1988) *Setting Up and Operating a Business in Japan*, Tuttle, Tokyo.

Vogel, E F (1985) *Japan as Number One: Lessons for America*, Tuttle, Tokyo.

—— (ed) (1981) *Modern Japanese Organization and Decision-Making*, Tuttle, Tokyo.

Whitehill, L, Arthur, M (1991) *Japanese Management: Tradition and Transition*, Routledge, London and New York.

Wolferen, Karel van (1990) *The Enigma of Japanese Power: People and Politics in a Stateless Nation*, Macmillan (Papermac), London.

Woronoff, J (1985) *The Japan Syndrome*, Yohan, Tokyo.

Yomiuri Shimbun (1991) *Meeting the Challenge of Global Leadership*, 21st Yomiuri Symposium on the International Economy, guidelines and position paper, Tokyo.

Young, A K (1989) *The Sogo Shosha: Japan's Multinational Trading Companies*, Tuttle, Tokyo.

CULTURE (AND ART)

Barnlund, D C (1975) *Public and Private Self in Japan and The United States: Communicative Styles of Two Cultures*, Simul Press, Tokyo.

—— (1989) *Communicative Styles of Japanese and Americans. Images and Realities*, Wadsworth, Belmont, CA.

Ben-Dasan, I (1989) *The Japanese and The Jews*, translated from the Japanese by R L Gage, Weatherhill, Tokyo.

Christopher, R C (1989) *The Japanese Mind: The Goliath Explained*, Tuttle, Tokyo.

Condon, J C (1990) *With Respect to the Japanese*, foreword by Kohei Goshi, Yohan, Tokyo.

Hendry, J (1986) *Marriage in Changing Japan: Community and Society*, Tuttle, Tokyo.

Keene, D (1981) *Appreciations of Japanese Culture* (previously published as *Landscapes and Portraits*) Kodansha, Tokyo.

Nakamura, Takafusa (1985) in Zusammenarbeit mit Bernard R G Grace *Wirtschaftliche Entwicklung des modernen Japan*, Ministerium fuer Auswaertige Angelegenheiten, Japan.

Reischauer, E O (1989) *The Japanese Today: Change and Continuity*, Tuttle, Tokyo.

—— (1988) *Japan Past and Present*, Tuttle, Tokyo, 3rd edn.

Salmon, P (1985) *Japanese Antiques With a Guide to Shops*, Art International Publishers, Tokyo.

White, M (1990) *The Japanese Educational Challenge: A Commitment to Children*, Kodansha, Tokyo.

GENERAL REFERENCE (UNIVERSAL)

JETRO (1991) *Investment Japan 1991–92*, a Directory of Institutions and Firms offering assistance to people seeking to set up business in Japan, Tokyo.

Royal Mail International Business Travel Guide (1990) Columbus Press, London.

HISTORY

Beasley, W G (1990) *The Rise of Modern Japan*, Tuttle, Tokyo.

JOB HUNTING AND LIVING IN JAPAN

British Chamber of Commerce, Science and Technology Group (1990) *Gaigin Scientist: How to find a research post in Japan and what it's like when you get there*, Tokyo.

Brockman, T (1991) *The Job Hunter's Guide to Japan*, Kodansha, Tokyo.

Community House and Information Centre (Kobe) edited by Mary Kitson (1989) *Living in Kobe 1989*, Kobe, Japan.

Davidson, R (1990) *Living and Working in Japan*, Yohan, Tokyo.

De Mente, B (1982) *The Tourist and the Real Japan. How to avoid pitfalls and get the most out of your trip*, Tuttle, Tokyo.

JETRO (1990) *Establishment of a Representative Office in Japan – A Guide for Foreign Businessmen*, Tokyo.

LANGUAGE

The Association for Overseas Technical Scholarship (1990) *ACTS: Practical Japanese–English Dictionary*, Tokyo.

Hiroo Japanese Center (1989) *The Complete Japanese Verb Guide*, Tuttle, Tokyo.

Martin, S E (1989) *Easy Japanese: A Direct Approach to Immediate Conversation*, Tuttle, Tokyo.

Matsumoto, M (1988) *The Unspoken Way – Haragei: Silence in Japanese Business and Society*, Kodansha, Tokyo.

Mizutani, O and N, Nihongo notes vols 1–5, *The Japan Times*, Tokyo:
Vol 1 (1990) *Speaking and living in Japan*
Vol 2 (1991) *Expressing oneself in Japanese*
Vol 3 (1990) *Understanding Japanese usage*
Vol 4 (1990) *Understanding communication in Japanese*
Vol 5 (1990) *Studying Japanese in context*

—— Situational Japanese vols 1–5, *The Japan Times*, Tokyo:
Vol 1 (1990)
Vol 2 (1990)
Vol 3 (1990)
Vol 4 (1991)
Vol 5 (1990)

—— (1984) 'Japanese: The Spoken Language in Japanese Life', translated by Janet Ashby, *The Japan Times*, Tokyo.

Passin, H (1977) *Japan and the Japanese*, Kinseipo, Tokyo.

Sei, R (1990) *Crash Japanese for Businessmen Survival!* (just 40 hours! Imaginative! with cassette!) temporary Center Persona Education Bonjinsha Co, Ltd, Tokyo.

Seward, J (1985) *Japanese in Action*, Weatherhill, New York.

LITERATURE

Mikes, G (1970) *The Land of the Rising Yen*, Penguin, London.

Sugimoto, Etsu Ignagaki (1985) *A Daughter of the Samurai*, Tuttle, Tokyo and Vermont.

Tanizaki, J (1989) *The Makioka Sisters,* translated from the Japanese by E G Seidensticker, Tuttle, Tokyo.

FINANCE

National Westminster Bank PLC *Private Banking Services – NatWest Tokyo Branch* (Information Sheets), Tokyo.

Social Insurance Agency *Employees' Pension Insurance System Established in Japan for your joining*, Tokyo.

VIDEOCASSETTES AND FILMS

B & C I Inc (1989) *The Tradition of Performing Arts in Japan: The Heart of Kabuki, Noh and Banraku*, Nippon – The Land and its People Video Series (English version), Tokyo.

British Chamber of Commerce, *You Can't Afford to Ignore Japan*, Tokyo.

JETRO (the following 16mm films can be borrowed, subject to availability):

A Commitment to Harmony
How to Enjoy Making Good Products – An Introduction to QC Activities
The Japanese Consumer
The Music Maker – Portrait of a Small Business
Bridges and Barriers

NHK Enterprises Inc/Sogovision Inc, Videocassette series *Anatomy of Japan: The Wellsprings of Economic Power:*

1. Postwar Japan: 40 Years of Economic Recovery (60 min)
2. Postwar Japan: 40 Years of Economic Recovery (narrated in Japanese) (60 min)
3. An Economy in Transition: Japanese Business Goes Abroad (60 min)
4. An Economy in Transition: Japanese Business Goes Abroad (narrated in Japanese) (60 min)
5. The Shacho A Japanese President and his Company (45 min)
6. The Company Man: Myths and Realities of Lifetime Employment (30 min)
7. MITI: Guiding Hand of the Japanese Economic Miracle (30 min)
8. Small Companies: True Heroes of Japanese Industry (30 min)
9. Quality Control: An American Idea Takes Root in Japan (30 min)
10. A Test of Japanese Management: Japanese Cars Made in the USA (45 min)
11. Breaking Barriers: Foreign Companies that succeed in Japan (30 min)
12. Japan and the Future: A Time for Choice (45 min)

Sogavision Inc also published a handbook to accompany the above called *Anatomy of Japan* (1987), Tokyo.

Index

TITLES OF INTEREST IN
BUSINESS AND BUSINESS TRAVEL

For further information or a current catalog, write:
NTC Business Books
a division of *NTC Publishing Group*
4255 West Touhy Avenue
Lincolnwood, Illinois 60646-1975 U.S.A.

2721